THE REBELLIONS OF ISRAEL

THE REBELLIONS OF ISRAEL

ANDREW C. TUNYOGI

JOHN KNOX PRESS
Richmond, Virginia

Scripture quotations are from the Revised Standard Version, copyright 1946 and 1952 by the Division of Christian Education of the National Council of the Churches of Christ in the U.S.A.

In the preparation of this book the author used his article "The Rebellions of Israel," which was published in the *Journal of Biblical Literature*. Vol. LXXXI, Part IV, 1962, and is used by permission.

Standard Book Number: 8042-0165-X
Library of Congress Catalog Card Number: 69-19471
© M. E. Bratcher 1969
Printed in the United States of America

TO THE MEMORY
OF MY DAUGHTER
ANN

CONTENTS

1. Introduction   11

2. The Motif of the Rebellions of Israel in the
   Tetrateuch   33

3. The Emergence of the Rebellion Motif in History   57

4. The Meaning of the Rebellion Motif   77

5. The Rebellion Motif Outside the Tetrateuch   97

6. The Significance of the Rebellion Motif for the
   New Israel   125

   Notes   147

THE REBELLIONS OF ISRAEL

1

INTRODUCTION

This book is an attempt to call attention to a particular conviction underlying some stories in the Tetrateuch. The conviction is that Israel from the time she was elected as the people of the Lord in Egypt repeatedly rebelled against him, yet was never utterly rejected but was forgiven and kept in the communion of the covenant. The present writer believes that this conviction is unique in the Old Testament and has no parallel in other religions; yet it has not received the attention it deserves from biblical scholars.

The conviction is unique in the history of religions because both of its elements, the sin committed by Israel and God's response to it in grace, are uniquely Israelite. As students of comparative religion assure us,[1] in ancient times sin was not conceived of as a mere moral offense, entailing punishment; sin resulted in the loss of the life-giving and life-promoting power which came from the divine. This idea is well known also in the Old Testament (Deut. 28-30; 1 Sam. 16:14; Pss. 32:3 ff.; 90:7 ff.[2]) and, just as in other religions, if the sin was not too great, the power could be restored by cultic rites. But the sin of rebellion should have resulted in total loss of the power. All stories dealing with it speak of an incurable breach of the communion, a destruction of the Lord's covenant, which should have severed the bond between the Lord and Israel and cut off the flow of life to her. The result should have been that "curses shall come upon you and pursue you and overtake you, till you are destroyed" (Deut. 28:45). The sin of rebellion is not ethical; it is not the violation of moral principles binding all humans, as, for example, the principle that no harm should be done to one's own self or others; neither is it violation of divine commandments or neglect of one's duties.[3] It is a sin which creates a situation where the following of moral principles or the keeping of divine commandments loses meaning because Israel is outside the divine realm. Yet, although not ethical sin, it is willful destruction of a relationship on which everything—the nation's life, its welfare, its very existence—depends. In the stories of the Tetrateuch its seriousness is heightened by three characteristics: First, it is deliberate, committed in full consciousness; second, it is done collectively by the entire people; third, it is repeated over and over again. We find no parallel of such a sin in the environment of ancient Israel. When Mesha speaks about Chemosh, the god of the Moabites, being angry at his people,[4] this is apparently because of an unconscious sin. In Mesopotamia, dynasties were destroyed by the gods because one of their members, but not the whole people, offended them.[5]

The second motif of the rebellion stories, that the Lord's response to this deadly sin was grace, is also uniquely Israelite. For other nations the idea of such divine grace was unthinkable because their gods were so closely bound to them that the destruction of the nation would have also meant the death of the gods. Israel's God, however, could exist without Israel, and the destruction of the covenant would have entailed the death of Israel only. Thus the conviction that God forgives even the ultimate sin over and over again is unique, and shows the falsity of the popular belief that the God of the Old Testament is a vengeful God while that of the New Testament is merciful. It shows that God's face in both Testaments is the same. It is the face of the forgiving, loving Father who does punish—but behind the punishment there is always the will to save.

Yet, despite its uniqueness and obvious significance, the conviction has not received the attention it deserves. This is true even of those two scholars who made a new approach to the interpretation of the Old Testament, Gerhard von Rad in Germany and G. Ernest Wright in this country. Both hold that the Old Testament—and for that matter, also the New Testament—speaks about the saving acts of God as seen by Israel in history. According to von Rad, the so-called Hexateuch (the first six books of the Old Testament, Genesis-Joshua) is an expanded confession, a *credo,* about the saving acts of God in the past, beginning with the patriarchs and ending with the conquest of Canaan, to which the Deuteronomic History (consisting of the books Judges-2 Kings) added the story of the fulfillment of God's promises under David.[6] In a later book, von Rad deals again with the problem, and stresses, both in the historical books and in the prophets,[7] the *kerygmatic* (i.e., proclamatory) nature of the Old Testament story. He describes the proclamatory history as "the result of Israel's thinking about herself, a process which was constantly operative in the history," and believes that this thinking was necessitated because each generation "was faced with the ever-identical yet ever-new task of understanding itself as Israel."[8] Wright, writing before the publication of von Rad's later book, accepted the opinion of the German scholar and described biblical faith as history interpreted by faith.[9] Building on the results of von Rad, he distinguishes five "events" in the Old Testament story which constitute the center of faith: the "events" of the patriarchs, the exodus, the covenant at Sinai, the conquest of Canaan, and the "event" of David.[10]

These ingenious insights of the two scholars are important and, by and large, true. It is true that Old Testament history is confessional, i.e., that its main intent is not to tell actual history but to proclaim beliefs; that it reflects a constantly

recurring endeavor of successive generations to reinterpret
themselves as Israel, the people of the God of the patriarchs
and of Sinai; it is true that in the historical books, "events,"
demonstrating particular elements of faith, are the most conspicuous. Perhaps only one minor objection could be made
against von Rad's attempt to derive Old Testament history
writing from a credo and against the use of the term within
Old Testament scholarship. Although he does not say so, the
case probably is that the idea and the term were borrowed
from New Testament scholarship, which, as is generally
known, uses the term *kerygma* to denote the New Testament
message. As von Rad believes, it was the Old Testament confession of ancient times, as expressed in cultic recital, out of
which Old Testament history writing grew.[11]

It is much better, however, and considering the centrality
of the cult in Israel, easier and more natural, to see the roots
with Claus Westermann in praise.[12] The Psalms quoted by
von Rad (78, 105, 138) are examples of primitive history in
the form of praise. Even the passage in Deuteronomy 26:5 ff.,
quoted as primary evidence for von Rad's thesis, is not a confession but a proclamation of the saving acts of God, i.e., not
credo but praise. Then the term creates confusion. To be
sure, the proclamatory biographies in the New Testament, the
Gospels, grew out of the confession, "Jesus is the Christ."
They explained and proved why he must be accepted as the
Christ, the Messiah of Israel. This creedal act was made necessary by the fact that, historically speaking, Christianity was
one of the oriental cults broken off and freed from its native
soil, Judaism, and thus made universal. Such separation of
cults from their mother religions, by which they acquired
appeal for all nations, was a common phenomenon in the
Hellenistic age, as is shown by Mithraism and the cult of Isis,
to mention only the two best-known cases. Membership in
these cults called for a decision expressed in a confession, and

Christianity was not an exception. In Israel, and for that matter in Judaism, there was no need for a credo expressing decision. The Israelite was born into the Lord's people; he could make no decision for God, only against him, because the decision had already been made for him by Abraham. The Israelite could only express the joy of his belonging to God, already real, and that expression necessarily took the form of praise.

Yet, in spite of their true and important insights, neither von Rad nor Wright deals with the motif of Israel's rebellions. The former mentions it only peripherally.[13] Why this neglect? As the present writer sees it, both scholars were arrested by a specific view of Old Testament literary history suggested almost irresistibly by the historical books themselves in their present form. In interpreting the Old Testament, it was, therefore, difficult for them to take into consideration a fact of literary history familiar to all since the time of the Graf-Wellhausen school: the fact that the historical books were compiled during or after the captivity for a particular, practical purpose and were not simply the results of a process of growth. The mere literary growth is so strongly suggested by the present texts that under their influence a theory was developed around the middle of the nineteenth century that the process began sometime under David or Solomon and ended after the Babylonian exile. This theory is by and large true. As a result of the biblical research carried on since the middle of the nineteenth century, it became increasingly clear that there were ancient traditions in Israel; that these traditions, either in written or oral form, or perhaps in the form of expansions of various writers, grew more and more extensive throughout the centuries; and that many of the traditions were eventually combined in the three great historical works of the Old Testament, the Tetrateuch (Genesis-Numbers; according to others the Pentateuch, Genesis-Deuteronomy, or the Hexateuch, Genesis-

Joshua), the Deuteronomic History, and the work of the Chronicler. At any rate, at the end of the nineteenth century, this theory was accepted by Graf and Wellhausen as valid for the Tetrateuch (according to them, the Pentateuch), but they made an important correction. They proved that, contrary to previous opinion, the priestly material was the most recent among the three or four "documents" or strands in the Tetrateuch[14] (J, E, P, and D) and that a priestly author who lived after the exile was responsible for the present form of the Tetrateuch.

This view, known as the Graf-Wellhausen hypothesis, was generally accepted, but their important discovery that the Tetrateuch in its present form was completed after the exile was not sufficiently utilized in the work of interpretation. It was not fully realized that the Tetrateuch was not compiled merely to preserve the memory of the past, but was rather a work with a definite tendency. The truth of Sandmel's statement was not clearly seen: *"No writer ever writes without some purpose."*[15] To accept this statement with all its implications means to accept that the Tetrateuch was the result not only of the forward movement of tradition but also of a backward movement made by the final redactor who selected from the traditional material that which served his purpose. This purpose must be taken into consideration in the work of interpretation.

The nature of the Tetrateuch is made more plausible if we consider that all historical works in the present Old Testament had a pragmatic purpose. As was just mentioned, besides the Tetrateuch there are two other historical works, the Deuteronomic History (containing all books from Deuteronomy to 2 Kings) and the work of the Chronicler (1, 2 Chronicles, Ezra, Nehemiah). Their order is not chronological in the Old Testament, their relative age being rather Deuteronomic History, Tetrateuch, and work of the Chronicler. The first was completed ca. 550, the second ca. 400, the third ca. 300 B.C. Whatever the date of the material incorporated into them may have been, one thing is certain: At the time of the compilation each final editor had a particular purpose in mind, had a message that he endeavored to bring home to his generation, and in doing so proclaimed particular convictions. Can their purposes and convictions be detected in their works?

To begin with the latest of the works, the purpose and the convictions are easiest to see in the work of the Chronicler. His purpose was to justify the claim of the returnees from Babylonia against the claims of other Israelite groups that the Jerusalem community alone was the legitimate heir to pre-captivity Israel. In order to do this he made use of a Deuteronomic belief that whenever a total breach occurred between the Lord and his people (or whenever there was need to strengthen the relationship between them), the making of a new covenant, or rather a repetition of the covenant, was demanded. As the Chronicler believed, the covenant ceremony under Ezra and Nehemiah was the last in the series of covenant repetitions and was just as valid as the previous acts of this nature.[16]

The purpose of the Deuteronomic History is not difficult to find either. Using for his work material dating as far back as the time of David and Solomon, the compiler wrote in order to prepare his people for the restoration after the exile. In doing so, he told the story from the time when Israel arrived opposite Jericho till the elevation of King Jehoiakin by his Babylonian overlord in the captivity. His most conspicuous conviction was that disloyalty to the Lord always brought disaster. Illustrating it with the stories of both Israelite and Judean kings, he warned that such sin should never be committed again.

The third (chronologically, the second) great work, the Tetrateuch, had the same purpose as the Deuteronomic History: to give a design for restored Israel after the captivity. In doing so, its author proclaimed certain convictions, and by them he endeavored to establish beyond doubt that "Israel" (meaning probably not only the Jerusalem community[17]) alone was the people chosen by God for the good of all mankind; to show that the community of the restoration had full right to the land of Israel; to encourage them in the belief of divine protection; to give in the law a detailed design for the life within the divine realm; and, as a means of reconciliation, to reestablish the cultic system.

Of course, in producing his work each of the three compilers followed a particular line of theology determined by his age and his religious and cultural environment. Each had, therefore, differing opinions concerning Israel's self-understanding, her life and institutions. In other words, they held different religious convictions, and their purpose was to proclaim these convictions in their works. This view about the origins of the three works leads us to two conclusions. First, that only one or perhaps a very few individuals are responsible for the final form of the works; second, that in order to put forth their convictions the compilers made selections in the material available to them. What we have now before us represents the theology, religion, and opinions of the final redactors, and it was their convictions that determined the material they preserved. They stood at certain points of history, and in considering the needs of their own age, moved backward in the history of their people, selecting only particular elements of tradition, written or unwritten, which they found adequate for expressing their convictions.

Of course, this view does not and cannot deny the forward movement of tradition. It does not deny that the interpretation of history began with the recitation of the Lord's saving acts in cultic praise, that history writing commenced under David and Solomon, that, as von Rad tells us, it was reinterpreted over and over again, and that from time to time new elements were added to the interpretation. It does not and cannot deny the existence of successive redactors, even if they followed each other in a rather complicated manner, as Eissfeldt believes,[18] nor does it challenge the theory of Sandmel concerning haggadic growth. It leaves the door fully open to further research in the forward movement of tradition and literary growth. This view simply states that when it comes to interpretation, the last redactor, his age, his environment, his purpose, and his convictions always have to be kept in mind, and if there is material incorporated in his work expressing convictions which it seems implausible he should hold, that material still has to be interpreted in the light of his convictions. It means, for example, that it would be senseless to work out the theology of the Yahwist and the views of the priestly editor independently and set the differences against each other. For the purpose of interpreting the Tetrateuch, "the theology of the Yahwist" should be seen and understood only in the light of the priestly editor, and presented as his views. After all, he adopted the J material, and he did so because he agreed with the beliefs behind it.

Sandmel's other remark, that the author of the Tetrateuch was not a "moron" and that "he was highly selective in the bits and pieces which he utilized,"[19] is also true. Undoubtedly the redactor of the Deuteronomic History and the Chronicler were not morons either. One may even risk an opinion that the continuity and independence of the Yahwist narrative appear to us to be such because the last editor of the Tetrateuch selected his material in a sequence to fit not the Yahwist's narrative but his own. Who can find the truth here? To find it, it would be necessary to ask the priestly editor himself. But this is now impossible. For the purpose of interpretation, therefore, we must be satisfied with his work as it stands before us.

This is not the place to go into detail regarding the

Deuteronomic History and the work of the Chronicler. It would be possible also to extract from their works their particular convictions, but, since we intend to deal with the motif of Israel's rebellions, which is most conspicuous in the Tetrateuch, we will concern ourselves with this work. Setting aside for the time being the motif of the rebellions, the following are the main themes and convictions proclaimed in the Tetrateuch:

1. The election of Israel in Abraham gave an opportunity to all nations to join the realm of God by blessing themselves with the name of Abraham.

2. The land of Canaan belongs to Israel, represented by the patriarchs, particularly Abraham the father of nations, to whom it was given by a covenantal promise.

3. God protects Israel as he protected the forefathers and the nation during the forty years in the wilderness.

4. The Lord loves Israel, and his might is incomparable. He showed his love when he delivered Israel from Egypt and demonstrated his might in defeating the pharaoh.

5. Israel, i.e., Abraham, multiplied and became God's people by sheer grace through the covenant at Sinai.

6. At Sinai, a design of life pleasing to God was given in the law. Because this design is divine, only that life is truly human and worthy of living which complies with it.

7. Since by the covenantal blood Israel received the quality of holy life, holiness must be restored to her individual members if, either by becoming defiled by alien holiness (i.e., impurity) or by violating the law, that holiness was weakened. To serve as a means of restoring holiness, the cult was established; it must be performed in the tabernacle and by the priesthood planned and instituted by God through Moses. There were also feasts established when the people were collectively nurtured by God's holiness, the sacred life deriving from him.[20]

Of course, in dividing the Tetrateuchal material according to themes and convictions, complete accuracy is not possible. Some of the themes overlap and are built inseparably into the same story—e.g., the ordinance of the Passover is embedded in the story of the deliverance from Egypt (Exodus 12:1-28). Others are only loosely connected with the main themes. For example, the story of the creation of the world, the place where God and man will live in communion, is a prelude to the story that leads up to Abraham's election; and the story of Lot (Gen. 19) and the genealogy of Esau (Gen. 37)—neither of them essential for the main themes—are inserted into the saga collection about Abraham. As far as the convictions are concerned, the story of the deliverance from Egypt could also be joined to the protection passages. Any attempt to make a perfect division according to the convictions is futile because the final redactor did not intend to give a systematic presentation of the themes and convictions. He perhaps could not even list them as they were listed above. Yet anyone who takes the time to go through the entire material, although he may disagree with the details, will admit that all material can be classified under one of these themes, except the rebellion stories.

The convictions mentioned above were crystallized during Israel's troubled history, and they always had a significance. Since they spoke to the people in ever-changing historical situations, they probably did not always have the same form. It is impossible to reconstruct them as they were heard by successive generations, yet in the mediation of the Tetrateuchal author, each of these convictions both perfectly fitted his historical situation and had a specific message. The formation of the Tetrateuch in its present form began sometime in the last years of the exile, and its author lived around 400 B.C. For the generations of this (roughly) one century, the tradition of Abraham's election proclaimed the special standing of Israel which was to be restored, and called upon all his descendants to separate themselves from other nations and to unite.

The divine promise concerning the land was also important.

At that time new Canaanites were in possession of the land. Unlike the Chronicler, the Tetrateuchal author probably did not view the descendants of the northern tribes, the Samaritans, as aliens. His aim was not to divide but to unite, and, after all, the Samaritans were also descendants of the old Israel. For some time they were the dominant group, and it is even probable that Jerusalem was part of the Persian province, Samaria.[21] But the Samaritans were not the only "Canaanites" in the land. There were also Arabs, Ashdodites,[22] and almost certainly Moabites and Edomites (Ps. 137:7; Lam. 4:21 f.; Ezek. 25:12). In this context it is understandable why stories and genealogies of Lot and Esau were adopted. In speaking about the ancestors, the author also spoke about their descendants Moab, Ammon, and Edom, and expressed the hope that sometime they also would belong to "Israel." He also believed that the promise about the dispossession of the ancient Canaanites was an archetypal precedent, and the present "Canaanites" would just as certainly be dispossessed by the Lord as those of ancient times had been.

The proclamation of the belief that God had protected the ancestors and had once delivered Israel from Egypt also had its encouraging message. It promised divine intervention and help to the generation of the restoration, which in the undoubtedly precarious situation of the author's time was necessary. By his time the tradition of the Sinai covenant, and whatever went with it, was indispensable to any group considering itself part of Israel. But this was not the only reason why the author recorded it faithfully. Its three main elements—the election of Israel, the law, and the cult—were the main foundations of restored Israel. The first reinforced the comforting message of Abraham's election, the second gave a divine order of life to the people, and the third served as an always available means of restoring communion with the Lord. And of course they also distinguished sharply between the resurrected nation of God and all other nations.

If it is accepted that the purpose of the Tetrateuch was to present a design for restoration after the national tragedy and that its author endeavored to encourage the group charged with the restoration, the work of interpretation will be easier and its result will be more relevant for the preaching and teaching of the church today. Perhaps an objection could be raised that such a view is too primitive, and that if it is true, we would find exhortations in the text not unlike the exhortations in Deuteronomy. But if we will consider the method of preaching and teaching in those ancient times, we will understand the Tetrateuchal author. He lived in an age when the method of preaching was telling stories. The myth, whose atmosphere the author breathed, used the same method, and the stories of the Tetrateuch, of course in a specific Israelite manner, functioned very much like the myth, as we shall see. Besides, he was a "scholar." For him, therefore, the stories and the convictions expressed by them were more important than plain exhortations. Another objection might be that if the author's aim was to give a design for restoration, he would have written more of his own views. There are a few passages which are of this cast, but the author mainly used ancient material. This is not strange, for like the redactors of the two other historical works, he was a son of Israel and his thought and beliefs were permeated by the traditions shaped before the exile. He believed he was simply presenting ancient history, and did not fully realize that by making selections in the material and by shaping it into the present pattern he was creating something new. However, he omitted much material of which there are now only traces. We cannot tell whether the rest of the fragmentary myth in Genesis 6:1 ff. was omitted by the Yahwist or by him. Or, if it is indeed true that there was a New Year festival in pre-captivity Israel in which the Davidic king played a mythological role,[23] whether our redactor omitted it because that festival was the expression of a belief which he could not accept. Finally, we might wonder why there are no references to the contemporary situation. As it seems, he wanted his work to appear ancient—and as far as most of its material was concerned, it was that indeed. For this reason there is no mention of either the exiles or the returnees. For him the didactic purpose was important—the conclusions that could be drawn by his audience—and therefore he neglected to give information about the contemporary situation.

So far, we have set aside the theme of Israel's rebellions. In turning to it now, it must be stressed that this theme stands out clearly only if one classifies the material of the Tetrateuch not according to documents, strands, or groups of tradition, but according to themes and convictions—that is, if one takes into account not only the forward movement of tradition and literary growth but also the backward movement of the redactor, his selective activity in the old material. If this classification is made, the stories demonstrating the rebellion motif are left unclassifiable under any other theme. Thus, being unclassifiable they create a problem and ask for investigation.

This view of Old Testament history writing and interpretation raises several questions. One concerns the subject of Old Testament theology. Von Rad holds that its object should not be what scholars have found out about the Old Testament and its beliefs, but what Israel said about the Lord in faith.[24] This view can be accepted, but if the present writer's view is also accepted, i.e., that all three historical works in the Old Testament are writings which tend toward certain goals and are the results of an activity which made selections from old material, then it is not Israel that speaks in them but the final redactors. Another question is raised by Walther Eichrodt. As he admits, and as is generally known, a wide chasm already exists between the results of Old Testament scholarship and the convictional and proclamatory history of the Old Testament. Eichrodt charges, "In von Rad's preliminary methodological remarks (I, pp. 111 ff.) this rift is wrenched apart with such violence, on the basis of the preceding historical sketch (I, pp. 13 ff.), that it seems impossible henceforward to restore any inner coherence between these two aspects of Israel's history."[25] Does not the view presented by the present writer make the chasm even wider?

These difficulties are indeed real and they must be faced. To both of the questions I answer that since all three great historical works are works with tendencies toward a religio-national restoration, in the work of interpretation this fact cannot be neglected regardless of what it entails for Christian theology.

As for the first problem—that if we take this view, we do not hear Israel's voice but the voices of the individual redactors—what has already been said above should be repeated: The redactors were the sons of Israel, and in selecting their material they did not do so according to totally new beliefs. They were guided by old beliefs except that they shaped these beliefs according to the demand of the circumstances. Through their mouths, therefore, Israel spoke in ever different situations by one of her members. As for the second problem—that my view makes the chasm between actual history and the convictional history as it appears in the Old Testament even wider than the view of von Rad—the answer must be affirmative. But this is unavoidable. One can go even farther and say that over and above the chasm between real history as re-created by scholars and convictional history (I call them sub-canonical and canonical histories; I used these terms in 1938 in an article published in the *Theologiai Szemle,* Debreczen, Hungary), we must reckon also with canonical and sub-canonical religion and literary history. By the first, I mean cases such as the sub-canonical religious practice of sacrificing the firstborn in Israel as against the canonical prohibition of the practice (Lev. 18:21; Deut. 18:10; Ezek. 20:26); by the second, I mean the literary history of the sources, documents, or oral tradition incorporated into the finished works and the literary history of the works themselves. But a sharp distinction between the canonical and sub-canonical layers does not mean the uprooting of Old Testament interpretation from history. After all, before a history interpreted by faith there must have been an actual history without interpretation. Eichrodt's endeavor to save "a real historical foundation for the faith in Yahweh" sounds like a residue of orthodoxy which still tries to maintain a perfect unity between the canonical and sub-canonical strata.

Another question can be asked with Eichrodt: Does all this mean, even more than the view of von Rad, that the Old Testament witness to Yahweh will lose its absolute uniqueness against the background of its religious environment? Of course it does, but as part of the universal history of religion, it never had such a uniqueness, and, moreover, it is not the only religion that has uniqueness. Certainly it has the unique feature that it sees the divine as appearing in history, but another unique feature—the divinity of cosmic life—belongs to Hinduism. In its Israelite form, the belief in a God appearing in history is without analogy, but the views of Greek speculative religion, commonly called Greek philosophy, are also unique.[26] The convictional statement of Eichrodt that the Old Testament witness is without analogy is true for him, for von Rad, and for many of us, but it is not true for a Buddhist. This is because *we* acknowledge that the living God spoke and created communion with Israel and—in the Christian context —with her successor, the early church, and is continuing to do so with us. One must, indeed, reinterpret the truth of revelation as understood in Christianity and admit that the biblical witness is "true" and valid not because the divine was found in history by Israel and the early church, but because the God who spoke there *for us* was the only true God, and he is bearing witness to himself in us by his Spirit.

Another charge of Eichrodt is that von Rad's view of the biblical witness as a series of new reinterpretations of history makes the systematic presentation of Israelite tenets of faith impossible. This charge may be even more legitimate when made against the view of the present writer. Remarkably, however, it is possible to make such a systematic presentation, which Eichrodt himself had demonstrated admirably. But, is it not, perhaps, the case that the presentation is possible not because the relation of God to man was conceived in the same basic way throughout Israel's history but because Old Testament literature, as it stands before us, is the creation of a few generations during some two and a half centuries (550-300 B.C.), and the authors, who were not too far from each other in time, selected and shaped their material according to their more or less similar convictions? It is generally admitted that in spite of many differences there are many basic similarities in the views of the Tetrateuch, the Deuteronomic History, the Chronicler, the prophetic collections, and the rest of the Old Testament writings. The view represented here does not make the systematic presentation of Israel's tenets of faith impossible; on the contrary, it makes it easier. Systematic presentation is possible because Old Testament literature was the product of a few generations during a period of a couple of centuries.

In this context the important book of John Bright, *The Authority of the Old Testament* (Nashville: Abingdon Press, 1967), should be mentioned. On the surface its primary concern appears to be the use of the Old Testament in the preaching of the church. As a work dealing with important problems of hermeneutics it is indeed a refreshing breeze in the arid land of our ways of preaching, and it is of such significance that it should be studied carefully by all who are responsible for the proclamation of the Word. It demonstrates that biblical scholarship is a vital function of the church, and that the biblical scholar is important also for the practical theologian.

This book is good hermeneutics because it is based on good biblical theology. But it is more than hermeneutics. We learn from Bright what biblical theology ought to be. If, as he says, the preacher's first task in preparing his sermon is to find the intended theology of his text (pp. 169 ff.), then we may conclude that the task of the biblical theologian, or the exegete, is to help him in this work. The biblical theologian labors not for the purpose of his own preaching, but lays the indispensable foundations of preaching. Good biblical theology is good hermeneutics and good hermeneutics is good biblical theology. The difference is in the viewpoint and in the method. This is not just a theory but it follows from the very nature of the Old Testament, and of the whole Bible, which does not "intend to provide us with historical and philosophical data . . . religious and ethical concepts" but intends "to make theological statements" (pp. 120-121). Old Testament theology, we may conclude, is the scholarly effort to find and to present the theological intentions of the Old Testment texts. This appears to be the position of Bright. Therefore, since it follows from the nature of the Bible, and since the definition and the method of all good science is determined by its subject matter, I believe that John Bright's position alone is acceptable within the church. And I also believe that if the position of Bright is consistently carried through by the Old Testament biblical theologian, the controversy between von Rad and Eichrodt and the concerns of the latter will lose their point.

There are many other ideas in Bright's book to which one is compelled to subscribe but which cannot be mentioned in a restricted space. I wish to point out only three, which seem to be the most important.

One is Bright's idea about the authority of the Bible. As he implies, it has authority only within the church. ". . . the Bible provides us with the primary, and thus the normative, documents of the Christian faith; it has, therefore, normative

authority . . . over all who claim to be Christians" (p. 30).
In our secular world (but when was this world not secular?)
this is a valid statement for all. The same thing of this statement can be said that has been said by Paul M. van Buren
about the resurrection. The statement that the Bible is authoritative for me, for us, "does not signify a movement from a
sense-content statement . . . to an empirical assertion," but
it "is verified by the conduct of the man who uses it."[27] In
other words, the Bible is authoritative only within the church,
the realm of the Spirit, who, in the last resort, is responsible
for its existence and authority. That authority is not subject to
external verification. For those who are "inside," it is verified
by the Spirit; for those who are "outside," the verification is
done by the conduct of those who are "inside." That conduct,
of course, includes also the pursuance of Old Testament
scholarly studies.

Another idea concerns the relation of the Old and New
Testaments. The unity of the two is, indeed, not in the fact
that the religions found in them are akin or that they preach
the same morality (which they do not) but in that both speak
about "a single redemptive process" (p. 140), or, as I like to
express it, in the fact that the New Testament is the direct
continuation of the Old Testament story.

The third thing to be pointed out is Bright's opinion
concerning the "essential features" of the Old Testament
structure of belief. They are, indeed, at least in the present
forms of the books, election, covenant, and eschatology, i.e.,
"a lively confidence in what God would do in the future" (pp.
131 ff.).

The present writer, therefore, has no argument with John
Bright. This book may be viewed as an attempt to bring into
focus one important "theological intention" of the Old Testament which, as will be pointed out in the last chapter, seems
to be relevant also for the New Testament people of God.

Examples of finding such intentions are given in Bright's book (Ch. V). Only three remarks are offered which, as far as I can see, would strengthen Bright's position.

First, if I am right in contending that the Tetrateuch, like the other two historical works of the Old Testament, was written to give a design for restored Israel after the captivity and to encourage the returnees in a hostile world, if its purpose was to proclaim and preach convictions—in Bright's language to "make theological statements"—then it turns out that the Tetrateuch was written precisely for the purpose for which it is used in the church. If this is true then Bright is more right than ever in what he says about Old Testament biblical theology.

Second, the present book may be viewed as an attempt to support Bright's statement that "there is an overarching unity in both Testaments" (p. 126). The motif of the rebellions of Israel has a theological intention which is not found in the New Testament, or found only on the periphery, yet which is in agreement with New Testament intentions.

Third, there is a statement in Bright's book with which, even though it expresses the opinion of practically all competent scholars, I hesitate to agree. The statement is that Israel's religion "had already in all essentials assumed its normative form in the earliest period of Israel's life" (p. 120). As I mentioned above, it seems that the authors of the "historical" works of the Old Testament—Deuteronomic History, Tetrateuch, Chronicler—although they compiled their works mostly from pre-exilic material, made selection in it according to their own beliefs. Here I may add that I believe the rest of the Old Testament books, in their *present* forms, were also created after the fall of Jerusalem in 587. If this is true, then the Old Testament books as they stand before us do not represent the early religion of Israel but the religion of the authors' age. By having made their selection in the material in accordance with that religion, the Old Testament authors succeeded in creating in us, late students of their works, the impression that Israel's religion was ready in all essentials from the earliest times on. As I see it, at this point a fundamental reconsideration of Old Testament interpretation, or theology, is called for.

This opinion, however, does not contradict anything said by Bright otherwise. It means only that in interpreting the Old Testament for the church one has to consider two viewpoints: first, of course, the viewpoint of the New Testament, but besides this, the viewpoint of Israel in the exile and in the post-exilic period.

2
THE MOTIF OF THE REBELLIONS OF ISRAEL IN THE TETRATEUCH

According to the present form of biblical tradition, the rebellions of Israel took place during the exodus from Egypt and during the forty years in the wilderness. Since the Tetrateuch deals with this period, we find all "original," i.e., traditionally authentic, forms of the stories there. There is only one original rebellion story not found in the Tetrateuch, to which Ezekiel makes reference. He does not tell the story itself but, quoting the Lord, says:

> And I said to them, Cast away the detestable things your eyes feast on, every one of you, and do not defile yourselves with the idols of Egypt; I am the LORD your God. But they rebelled against me and would not listen to me; they did not every man cast away the detestable things their eyes feasted on, nor did they forsake the idols of Egypt (20:7-8; cf. 23:1-4).

Perhaps he has in mind the tradition in Joshua 24:14 in its present context, but that is not certain. At any rate, what he is telling is not known to other Old Testament books. He says that Israel did worship the Egyptian gods, and when the Lord commanded that they separate from them, they did not obey. Besides Ezekiel, many books—Deuteronomy, the prophets, and some of the Psalms, particularly—refer to rebellions; all references, however, are to stories mentioned in the Tetrateuch. We are, therefore, concerned primarily with these stories. They are as follows:

1. Exodus 2:11-15. The refusal of Moses' mediation by an Israelite in Egypt struggling with his fellow.

2. Exodus 3-4. Moses' objections made to the Lord against being sent to deliver Israel from Egypt.
3. Exodus 5:19-21. The rebuke of Moses by the Israelite foremen.
4. Exodus 6:2-9. Moses' "second call" in Egypt and the people's refusal to listen to him.
5. Exodus 14:10-18. Israel's lack of confidence at the Reed Sea blaming Moses for bringing them out from Egypt.
6. Exodus 15:22-26. Marah, the healing of the bitter water.
7. Exodus 16 (Num. 11). The fleshpots. The complaint of the people about the lack of food, followed by the miracles of the manna and the quails.
8. Exodus 17:1-7 (Num. 20:1-13). Massah and Meribah, water from the rock.
9. Exodus 32. The golden calf.
10. Leviticus 10. Nadab and Abihu.
11. Numbers 11:1-3. Fire at Taberah.
12. Numbers 12. Miriam's revolt.
13. Numbers 13-14. The spies.
14. Numbers 16-17. Korah, Dathan and Abiram.
15. Numbers 21:4-9. The bronze serpent.
16. Numbers 25. The sin with Baal-Peor.

As was indicated above, the stories have two main themes: the rebellions of humans and the grace of the Lord. We shall deal with the themes separately. Among the rebellious humans there are two parties: Moses and Israel. Both are in close relationship with the Lord, and both resist his plan, although in a different manner. We shall deal, therefore, first with the rebellions of Moses, then with those of Israel.

Moses is prominent in the entire Old Testament. Perhaps only the figure of David could compete with him, but David's prominence is restricted to the Deuteronomic History, the book of Isaiah, and some of the Psalms. The Tetrateuch refers to him cryptically only in the story of Balaam (Num. 24:17), and the reference is not certain. Moses, on the other hand, appears frequently throughout the Old Testament, and the authority of his traditional figure is everywhere revered. Whether this image is historical or not is not important for the purpose of interpretation. It is generally admitted that this image is not accurate historically, although no competent scholar denies that he was an actual historical person, a man of flesh and blood. His Egyptian name in itself is a strong proof of his historicity. In ancient Egyptian language, it means "son." The present text derives it, mistakenly relying on popular etymology, from a Hebrew root and interprets it as meaning "one who was drawn out from water" (Exod. 2:10). But an Egyptian name could hardly have been invented for Moses by a tradition which, understandably, always had an anti-Egyptian tendency.

The unanimous witness of tradition about him is also evidence of his historicity. Had he never lived, a Mosaic tradition could never have been created and certainly not one that made him the foundation of everything truly Israelite. But, as happens with all important personages of history, Moses' figure was also overgrown with legends. To begin with, the story of his birth contains a legendary motif—the foundling of high origin and his eventual success—which was familiar throughout the ancient Near East and was told also about Sargon I, the Akkadian king.[1] His call at Sinai, his struggle with the pharaoh, and practically all the stories of the wilderness, even though there is some historical truth behind them, are legends and haggadic exaggerations. They can be recognized as such at first sight. There is no need to quote evidence of this point; whoever reads the stories of the Tetrateuch with objective eyes will readily admit this. To reconstruct an actual life story of Moses and draw a historically true design of his character would be an even more hopeless undertaking than to reconstruct the figure of the "historical Jesus." Yet such a personage could not be created from nothing.

There is, therefore, a very high probability—as this writer believes, a certainty—that Moses was indeed the leader of those Semitic clans which were enslaved by an Egyptian king, most probably Ramses II, and which were destined to become part of Israel. They left Egypt under his leadership, and he became later the chief of other pre-Israelite groups at Kadesh-barnea.[2] It is unfortunate that the details of his life and activities cannot be recovered; any speculation, interesting though it might be, is futile. For the purpose of interpretation, however, the legendary figure of Moses is important, not the historical facts about him. The author's intention was to bring home a message, to proclaim convictions, and therefore he shaped Moses' figure accordingly. If it is possible to analyze that figure properly, the message can be understood. Perhaps the author's language and means of expressing himself present difficulties for the modern reader, yet we must always keep in mind what the author intended to say. What are the elements and what is the meaning of Moses' traditional figure in the Tetrateuch?

In the Old Testament there are four important functionaries of the covenant: the prophet, the priest, the charismatic leader, and the judge. The kingship is not an office of its own kind, only a version of the charismatic leader, because in Israel, both in the North and in the South, this office was charismatic. The difference was that in the North, at least in theory, each king had to receive his charisma, i.e., the appointment and the ability to function as a king, individually from the Lord, whereas in Judah the king had to be a member of the charismatic dynasty of David. On the other hand, contrary to usual scholarly opinion, this writer believes that the judge's office was separate from all the rest. True, both kings and priests functioned also as judges, but their judicial function was conditioned by their specific office, the king being the supreme judge, and the priest the revealer of God's decision. But, as Exodus 18 and Numbers 25:5 show, the office of the judge was distinct from both the royal and the priestly functions. Moses, however, appears in all these four functions. He is called a prophet in a specific sense in Numbers 12:6 ff., and he receives the divine revelations as a prophet does, i.e., God seeks him, he does not seek God (Exod. 3). The stereotyped formula—"the Lord said to Moses"—is also prophetic. Deuteronomy even seems to believe that he was the first of the line of the prophetic succession, an unbroken line of prophets whom the Lord raised in every generation (Deut. 18:15 ff.). He is not called a priest (in the Old Testament he has this title only once, in Ps. 99:6), but he functions as a priest in offering the covenant-creating sacrifice (Exod. 24:5 ff.). Like other priests he is also the keeper of the sanctuary, the tent of meeting, the tabernacle, and he is a member of the priestly tribe, Levi. Though he has no royal title, he is a charismatic leader. He is the speaker for his people before the pharaoh, gives the command to leave Egypt, is the commander-in-chief when Israel meets her foes, and enforces the law (Exod. 11:4; 17:8 ff.; 32:25 ff.; Num. 21:32 ff.). Like all Israelite kings, he is also the depository of the royal power, and from him that power emanates for the destruction of the enemy (Exod. 17:11 ff.; cf. 1 Kings 22:35). Finally, he is also a judge (Exod. 18).

In all four functions he is more than an ordinary prophet, priest, charismatic leader, or judge. In Numbers 12, where his unique prophetic standing is challenged by Miriam and Aaron, the Lord's response to the challenge is:

> Hear my words: If there is a prophet among you, I the LORD make myself known to him in a vision, I speak with him in a dream. Not so with my servant Moses; he is entrusted with all my house. With

him I speak mouth to mouth, clearly, and not in a dark speech; and he beholds the form of the LORD (vss. 6-8).

In other words, Moses has prophetic status, a specific one; he is the "servant of the Lord," his grand vizier, and his "entrusted one" (Heb.) over his household, his steward or major-domo. Then, as a priest he is again more than an ordinary priest. He is a priest-maker; he is not only the keeper of the sanctuary but its builder, and not only dispenses occasional divine decisions, but also the totality of the divine law is given to Israel through him. His unique and never-to-be-repeated priestly standing is not weakened but strengthened by the statement of the Chronicler that his descendants were not counted among the priests but among the ordinary Levites (1 Chron. 23:14). Although as a charismatic leader he never fights, after he receives the command from the Lord he gives orders for the fight, and, which is important, he not only leads the people but through his mediation Israel becomes a nation. Lastly, his judgeship is also unique. As the already-quoted passage in Exodus 18 shows, he initiates the office in Israel, retaining only the right of the supreme judge, as befits kings (vs. 22; 2 Sam. 15:2 ff.; 1 Kings 3:16 ff.).

In addition to his standing as prophet, priest, charismatic leader, and judge, all four in a qualified sense, Moses is also a mediator of the Lord for the people, and of the people for the Lord. As a matter of fact, whenever he functions in any of the four offices, he is also a mediator in one direction or the other. His status as the Lord's representative is rooted entirely in the will and election of the Lord. The legend of his birth and miraculous deliverance from the Nile is told in order to teach this precept: The Lord was acting secretly in order to save the child given up in desperation by his mother. His call is also unusual. It comes unexpectedly at an age when, according to similar stories, such calls do not happen. He was eighty years old (Exod. 7:7) and settled for life among the Midianites.

Throughout his ministry he does not initiate anything positive but serves merely as the mouthpiece and instrument of the Lord. The struggle against the pharaoh is not his but the Lord's (Exod. 6:6 ff.), and that is eventually realized even by the Egyptian magicians (Exod. 8:19). He is not responsible for bringing Israel out of Egypt; neither are the murmurings of the people against him, but against the Lord (Exod. 6:6, 8; 17:2 ff., 7). His unique relation to the Lord is acknowledged in a rather unusual manner by the story of the golden calf, where the people tell Aaron:

> Up, make us gods, who shall go before us; as for this Moses, the man who brought us up out of the land of Egypt, we do not know what has become of him (Exod. 32:1b).

This implies that if Moses is not available, the Lord is not present either. Finally, the author thinks that, if he would have accepted it, Moses could have become equal to Abraham. Twice we are told that the Lord was ready to make him the root of a new people (Exod. 32:10; Num. 14:12).

Then, if Moses was the representative of the Lord to the people, he was also the representative of the people to the Lord. He assumed this function voluntarily. The author is careful to point out that even before his call and authorization by the Lord to be his messenger, Moses accepted solidarity with his people, even though he was a member of the pharaoh's household. The point of the story about killing the Egyptian who was beating a Hebrew (Exod. 2:11-15), an act that might be offensive to some of us, is that Moses was a hero ready to fight for his people on his own. Then, after he received his call, he interceded over and over again for his people with the Lord. Twice he prayed at the request of the people: once at Taberah when "the fire of the LORD burned among them, and consumed some outlying parts of the camp," and the other time when "the LORD sent fiery serpents among the people, and they bit the people, so that many people of Israel died" (Num. 11:1; 21:6).

These prayers must have appeared bold to all who read them in the time of the author. They tell us that Moses fearlessly reminded the Lord, a God of utmost sanctity (Num. 11:1; Lev. 10:2 ff.), of his own promises and saving acts, in effect telling him that he just could not go back on his word and act contrary to his own nature.[3] The bold prayers are topped by two acts, both bringing into sharp focus Moses' self-identification with his people. He twice refuses the offer of the Lord to make him the root of a new people after the destruction of rebellious Israel (Exod. 32:10b; Num. 14:12). The other act is his declaration that he is willing to die unless the Lord forgives Israel. In praying after the sin with the golden calf he says, "But now, if thou wilt forgive their sin—and if not, blot me, I pray thee, out of thy book which thou hast written" (Exod. 32:32).

All this—that Moses is a prophet, a priest, a charismatic leader, and a judge, in a qualified manner, that his authority is divine, and that he is the representative of the people—shows his unique significance in tradition. He is, indeed, *the* man of God (Deut. 33:1; Joshua 14:6; 1 Chron. 23:14; 2 Chron. 30:16; Ezra 3:2).

Considering the image of Moses drawn by tradition, one would expect that nothing but perfection could be ascribed to him. Yet the contrary is true. We are told that not only Israel but also Moses rebelled against the Lord.[4]

His first rebellion appears in the celebrated chapters of Exodus 3-4. As a rule, chapter 3 is thoroughly studied and diligently expounded because, as is believed, according to the Elohistic strand, the divine name Yahweh was revealed here for the first time, and no notice is taken that the passage has an entirely different point. If there is a passage in which the main point is the revelation of the hitherto unknown divine name, it is rather Exodus 6:2-3, originating in the circles of the author (P), while Exodus 3-4 speaks mainly about Moses' unwillingness to accept the divine commission to lead the people out of Egypt. These two chapters are built around four objections of Moses. The first objection of Moses is that he does not know the name of the God speaking to him, even though that God had identified himself as "the God of the fathers" and, as is assumed, must have been well known to Israel. This objection is overcome by the revelation of the unknown divine name, interpreted in a popular fashion.[5] The second objection is that Moses will be unable to give evidence that the Lord appeared to him (Exod. 4:1). Even though such difficulties never bothered other Old Testament prophets, our author tells that it was overcome by granting Moses miracle-working ability in filling his rod with power from the Lord. The third objection is childish. Moses says that he is not eloquent, whereupon he is told that the Lord will be with his mouth (vs. 12; Aaron, as the speaker for Moses, is a secondary motif in the story). Finally, the author reveals the real reason why Moses searches for excuses. His hero says: "Oh, my Lord, send, I pray, some other person" (vs. 13). In other words, Moses does not mind if the Lord delivers Israel, but wants no part in it. Why? We are not told. But the author probably had in mind the many difficulties he was about to relate and which Moses had to face. But on the unconditional divine command, Moses must go, anyway.

This initial unwillingness of Moses reappears in later stories, mostly in the forms of frustration and impatience. We find it in the story of the Israelite foremen. After they negotiated unsuccessfully with the pharaoh, and after they charged Moses that with his demand for Israel's release from Egypt he had worsened the lot of the people, their charge is turned by Moses against the Lord. In effect, he says that the Lord did not keep his word.

> O Lord, why has thou done evil to this people? Why didst thou ever send me? For since I came to Pharaoh to speak in thy name,

he has done evil to this people, and thou hast not delivered thy people at all (Exod. 5:22-23).

The P version of Moses' call also reports his unwillingness, although the objections are not given in the same details as in chapters 3-4 (Exod. 6:12, 30).

Then we find other rebellions. In Exodus 17:4 he only cries in desperation for help to the Lord, but in Numbers 11:11 he refuses to bear the burden of responsibility for the people alone. In verse 21 of the same chapter the motif is strengthened. In expressing his doubt that the Lord is able to feed with meat a people numbering six hundred thousand men of arms, Moses shows lack of confidence. The same sin, mistrust in the helping power of the Lord, reaches its culmination in Numbers 20:1-13. Its parallel in Exodus 17:1-7 (mainly J) says nothing about Moses' lack of faith, but the passage in Numbers—a haggadic expansion by P of the Exodus passage—although somewhat obscure, assumes that he did not believe in the Lord's ability to bring forth water from a rock. Instead of simply telling the rock, as he was directed by the Lord, "to yield its water" (Num. 20:8), he strikes it in impatience (vs. 11), whereupon the miracle happens. Then, as a punishment for his lack of confidence, the Lord declares that both he and Aaron must share the lot of the rebellious generation and cannot enter the promised land.

Why he was punished with such severity is difficult to see. Apparently the fact that Moses did not enter the promised land was a problem. Deuteronomic tradition (Deut. 1:37) assumes that he was identified by the Lord with the rebellious generation, although he himself was not guilty. Only the latest P tradition dared to attribute to him a lack of confidence. It changed somewhat the Massah-Meribah story as found in Exodus 17:1 ff. by adding the motifs of Moses' impatience and lack of faith. These two versions must have existed before the time of the author. He had access to both and found them sufficiently different to hold that they were about two different events. So he incorporated both into his work.

The unwillingness and impatience of Moses is in contrast with his obedience and unshakable confidence in other passages, as his confidence shown at the Reed Sea, his determination in the story of the spies (Exod. 14:13; Num. 13:20), and even more with the remark in Numbers 12:3 that he "was very meek, more than all men that were on the face of the earth." There was only one thing in which he was never shaken: his loyalty to the Lord. As we shall see, Israel was guilty in this respect, but Moses was always "jealous" for the Lord, even at the risk of his life (Exod. 32:26 ff.; Num. 14:10).

In what forms does the rebelliousness of the people appear? There are anticipations of future murmurings and rebellions even before the call of Moses. In Egypt the Hebrew man, beating his fellow, flatly refuses Moses' mediation. When he brings the promise of the Lord's deliverance, the people also are reluctant to listen to him, "because of their broken spirit and their cruel bondage" (Exod. 6:9). Later we find four forms of rebellion. First, murmurings because of lack of food and water (Exod. 15:24; 16; 17:1-7; Num. 11:1; 21:5); in haggadic exaggerations this appears as a demand for delicacies (Num. 11:4 ff.; 20:5b). Second, lack of confidence in the Lord's willingness and power to help against the enemy (Exod. 14:11 ff.; Num. 14:2). Third, idolatry (Exod. 32; Num. 25). The fourth form deals not with the dissatisfaction of the whole people but of groups of cultic personnel, and has specific points in mind. They are the story of Nadab and Abihu, the rebellion of Miriam, and the rebellion of Korah, Dathan and Abiram (Lev. 10; Num. 12; 16-17).

The first murmuring is for water at Marah, the second because of hunger in the story of the manna and the quails, the third at Massah-Meribah. The reason for the fourth complaint at Taberah is not told; only "misfortunes" are mentioned. Probably lack of water and food, or simply inconveniences are meant. All demonstrate the lack of confidence that the Lord is among them (Exod. 17:7b) or that he can help and provide for the people. In the book of Numbers the people's demand is for delicacies, for meat, vegetables, and fruit (Num. 11:4-5; 20:5). Something like this is indicated also in the story of the bronze serpent, where the people "loathe this worthless food," the manna. As is shown by a comparison between the story of the quails in Exodus 16:13, where it is mentioned briefly, and in Numbers 11:10 ff., where it is told in detail, and the contrast between Moses' obedience in Exodus 17:1-7 and his impatience and mistrust in the Lord in Numbers 20:2-13, the passages in Numbers are later haggadic expansions.

The second form of rebellion is lack of confidence that the Lord is willing and able to help against enemy forces. The first occurred immediately after the people left Egypt, at the Reed Sea, with the approach of the Egyptian troops. Here, referring perhaps to the charge of the foremen or the disbelief in the Lord's promise (Exod. 5:21; 6:9) or, more probably, to a now-lost bit of tradition, the people say,

> Is it because there are no graves in Egypt that you have taken us away to die in the wilderness? What have you done to us, in bringing us out of Egypt? Is not this what we said to you in Egypt, "Let us alone and let us serve the Egyptians"? For it would have been better for us to serve the Egyptians than to die in the wilderness (Exod. 14:11-12).

The motif appears in a much stronger form in the story of the spies. Here the people complain bitterly:

> Would that we had died in the land of Egypt! Or would that we had died in this wilderness! Why does the LORD bring us into this land, to fall by the sword? Our wives and our little ones will become a prey; would it not be better for us to go back to Egypt? (Num. 14:2-3).

They are ready to stone Moses and Aaron, break with the Lord, and return to Egypt. This is not a petty murmuring but open rebellion. It is the culmination of all complaints. The author, therefore, tells it in length, drawing his material from several versions. Moses' intercessory prayer for forgiveness of the sin is long and elaborate, and so is the Lord's condemnation, pronounced in lofty, prophetic style. The result is also most disastrous for the rebellious generation. Except for Caleb and Joshua, they cannot enter the promised land but must die in the wilderness.

The third form of rebellion is the greatest sin in Israel, idolatry. The first is the sin with the golden calf (Exod. 32), in which the whole people is guilty. This story is also long and elaborate, and is probably compiled from all three Tetrateuchal strands (JEP). There are a few points which the author wanted to stress. One is that the people were not immoral or godless. On the contrary. They were very religious. The request to Aaron, "Up, make us gods, who shall go before us," springs from a deep religious urge, felt much more keenly by ancient man than by us, our author included. What he really objects to is, therefore, found in the second half of the sentence: "as for this Moses, the man who brought us up out of the land of Egypt, we do not know what has become of him" (Exod. 32:1b). According to these words, as far as the god himself was concerned, it did not make much difference to the people whether he was the Lord, the God of Moses, or some other divinity.

Another point is Aaron's part in the story. According to the context, he was already the high priest of Israel, the top religious leader who was in charge of satisfying the religious needs of the people. In this capacity, he asks for the amulets of the people. Because of compiling two traditions, there is some confusion in the text; in verse 4 we are told that after receiving the gold, he "fashioned it with a graving tool," but the next words and Aaron's defense to Moses show what was really in mind. In verse 4 we are told that Aaron "made a molten calf"; in verse 24 he says that having obtained the gold of the amulets, "I threw it into the fire, and there came out this calf." That is, the golden statue of a calf was not made intentionally, neither was it the result of chance, but an act of some superhuman power, of a real god. Perhaps the idea is that since the idol was made from amulets, i.e., objects full of sacred power, that power, having been distributed previously in the amulets, manifested itself now in the form of a calf. If this is true, then the words of Aaron are perfectly justified, "These are your gods, O Israel, who brought you up out of the land of Egypt!" (vs. 4b). Supposedly this god had been with them all the time in the amulets, and now he revealed himself in the calf.

A third point is that as soon as the people began to worship the calf, the Lord rejected them. There is an emphasis on the divine words to Moses: "Go down; for *your* people . . . have corrupted themselves" (vs. 7; italics added). The characteristic Old Testament idea is clear: Israel must not worship any other gods but the Lord, the god of Moses, and if they do, they are not his people any more. This is why the Lord is ready to destroy them and make "a great nation" out of Moses (vs. 10). The total alienation of the people is acknowledged by Moses when he breaks the stone tablets, indicating that the covenant made shortly before is null and void.

The fourth point stressed is the role of the Levites. According to the story, "when Moses saw that the people had broken loose . . . then Moses stood in the gate of the camp," and at his call, "all the sons of Levi gathered themselves together to him" (vss. 25-26). Then, having been commanded to do so, they killed three thousand men, apparently the most determined rebels siding with the golden calf. This is obviously one of the traditions explaining the way Levi became the priestly tribe. There are other versions dealing with the same theme. Some hold that Levi was simply appointed by the Lord to be the priestly tribe (Num. 1:49; 3:5-10); another believes that the miraculous blossoming out of Aaron's rod made them priests (Num. 17:1 ff.). Two bits of tradition hold that they were offerings to the Lord. According to one, they served as redemption for the firstborn; according to the other, they were a "wave offering" by the people (Num. 3:44 ff.; 8:10 ff.). The tradition incorporated into the story of the golden calf holds that the Levites are priests because of their zeal for the Lord.

In the next chapter (Exod. 33) we find the fifth important point of the story. Originally it was an old (J? E?) tradition, independent of the tradition of the burning bush and the covenant-making in Exodus 19. It also told about the appearance of the Lord to Moses on Sinai and the subsequent establishment of the covenant. In its present context, however, it is a covenant-repetition—well known to the Deuteronomic History and the Chronicler (see note 16, ch. 1)—and the only one in the Tetrateuch. It has the same meaning as it has elsewhere: Since making and worshiping the golden calf totally destroyed the first covenant, there was need for a second covenant as a response to Moses' intercession.

The second rebellion by turning to an alien god is told by the story of the sin with Baal-Peor (Num. 25). The sin was participation in the fertility cult of that god by "sacred" promiscuity for the purpose of experiencing union with the divine in sexual frenzy. The story may have some historical truth in it; it may have preserved the memory that some Israelite clans turned to the Canaanite deity, Baal, even before the conquest. It is told here to serve as an example against the worship of this god, and, indeed, this story is quoted most frequently outside the Tetrateuch whenever struggle against baalism appears. Besides condemning baalism, it makes two important points. One is that it is telling about the "spotless generation" (cf. note 4, ch. 5) which, supposedly, was perfect. This is why only part of the people are represented as guilty, and why those who worshiped Baal-Peor were killed (vss. 4 ff.). The other point is the "praiseworthy" act of Phinehas. This is told to justify some sort of a privilege enjoyed by his descendants, probably the right to the high priesthood.

Finally, there is a group of rebellions in which only cultic personnel participated. They are the revolts of Nadab and Abihu, of the prophetess Miriam, sister of Moses, and the rebellion of Korah, Dathan and Abiram (Lev. 10; Num. 12; 16-17).

The rebellion of Miriam the prophetess (cf. Exod. 15:20) represents the rejection of uncontrolled prophetic intervention into the life of Israel.[6] What Moses' marriage with the Cushite woman has to do with his authority is hard to see, but as the story stands now, it speaks about Miriam's rejection of the absoluteness of that authority. Although in tradition Aaron became an accomplice secondarily, the charge is in the plural: "Has the LORD indeed spoken only through Moses? Has he not spoken through us also?" (Num. 12:2). The rebellion is not against priestly authority—Moses was not a priest in the ordinary sense—but against the unique representative of the Lord and, therefore, indirectly against the Lord himself. As has already been indicated, this story was told to establish beyond doubt that Moses was more than a prophet; he was the grand vizier and majordomo of his household. The legitimacy of the prophetic revelation is not denied (cf. Num. 11:26), but it is very definitely stated that it can never contradict or be accepted as superior to the revelation through Moses.

One of the two other rebellions of cultic personnel deals with unacceptable priestly rites, the other with the rebellion of a Levitic clan, Korah, and of some Reubenite clans.

The impermissible priestly rite, performed by the two sons of Aaron, Nadab and Abihu (Lev. 10), was that they "offered unholy [Heb., *not belonging, strange, alien*] fire." What the origin of this fire was is not clear, but it must have been taken either from the altar of an alien god or was ordinary fire not taken from the altar of burnt offering (Exod. 30:9; Lev. 16: 12; Isa. 6:6). Whatever the case might have been, the two sons of Aaron violated the commandments of the Lord concerning the rite. This is why the story is followed by lengthy precepts concerning priestly duties.

The other story, the rebellion of the Levitic clan Korah and of Dathan and Abiram, is much more complicated and longer (Num. 16-17). Two different stories are put together, one dealing with the rebellion of some Reubenites, descendants of the firstborn of Jacob, the other with the rebellion of the Korahite clan of Levi. The rebellion of the Reubenites may be old tradition (J?), whereas the Korah story is post-exilic. In the initiatory verses of Numbers 16, the author did his best to combine the two stories in a satisfactory manner. In 16:3b the charge is raised against Moses and Aaron that they "exalted" themselves over Israel (Hebrew uses a word implying self-exaltation to leadership); that is, Moses made himself supreme leader, Aaron high priest, illegitimately. In this one charge, the charges of the two groups, appearing originally in two different stories and having now been related to one another, are brought under a common denominator.

In 16:8-11 and 12-15, then, we learn the reasons for Korah's and the Reubenites' rebellions, and why they charged Moses and Aaron with usurpation of their offices. Korah desired the sharing of the priesthood with the Aaronides, and the Reubenites challenged Moses' unsuccessful leadership. In 16:25-35 we again find traces of the author's effort to combine the stories smoothly. Here Korah becomes the representative of both groups and the two are punished in the same way. But, because the author was a priest opposing the intention of the rebellious Levitic clan, Korah's rebellion was more important for him. He therefore added the story of Aaron's rod in chapter 17. It is a little awkward since it represents Aaron as standing for the entire tribe of Levi. Originally it was another, independent tradition about the election of Levi as the priestly tribe. In the present context, however, it is speaking for the priesthood of the Aaronides alone. At any rate, in the compilation of the author we now have a story, running more or less smoothly, which states that neither the supreme authority of Moses nor the sole right of the Aaronides to the priesthood can be challenged. Both rest on divine authority. The claim of the descendants of Reuben, Jacob's firstborn, to be the leaders of the nation must yield to the divine will and appointment. The same is true of the priesthood. If it was God's will to select only the Aaronides to be priests, the rest of the Levites must also yield.

There are two interesting points in the story. One is the joint statement of Korah, Dathan and Abiram that "all the congregation are holy, every one of them, and the LORD is among them" (16:3b). This is a claim, based on common possession of the holiness from God, asking for a sort of confused democracy, without visible human leadership. The other is that Aaron, the high priest of all the people, is willing, is able, and does make atonement for the rebellious people (16:46 ff.). That is, in spite of the rebellion against him, he does his duty for the sake of the guilty.

The rebellion stories of the Tetrateuch, however, speak not only about the sin of Moses, of the people, of Miriam, of the sons of Aaron, of the Levites and the Reubenites. They also speak about the reactions of the Lord. What were those reactions? In most cases it was punishment; but it was never utter destruction, especially not of the people as a whole. There is a tension between the divine anger and the divine mercy, yet his mercy, except in the stories dealing with the right to priesthood, is always greater.

Why was there an overflow of mercy? Certainly not because, according to the rebellion stories, the Lord was a sort of all-forgiving, fatherly type of God. There were three reasons for the divine forgiveness. The first and main reason was the Lord's faithfulness to his promise given the forefathers. Grace was overflowing because the Lord kept his word. After the introductory stories in Exodus 1-2 (the oppression of Israel and the birth and escape of Moses to Midian), our author presents this main theme, and that is going to determine everything he tells.

> In the course of those many days the king of Egypt died. And the people of Israel groaned under their bondage, and cried out for help, and their cry under bondage came up to God. And God heard their groaning, and God remembered his covenant with Abraham, with Isaac, and with Jacob. And God saw the people of Israel, and God knew their condition (Exod. 2:23-25).

The same theme reappears again and again throughout the Tetrateuch (Exod. 3:16 ff.; 6:6 ff.; 13:5 ff.; 32:13 f.; 33:1 ff.; Num. 15:1 f., etc.). With this the author proclaims: In making his promise to the fathers the Lord had set a goal for himself, and now he makes every effort to reach it. The stories of the rebellions show that the divine effort cannot be frustrated by human attitudes or resistance. In the entire course of the narrative there is not a single person—except, perhaps, Caleb and Joshua (Num. 14:6 ff., 24, 30; 26:65)—who would have agreed with the divine plan. With the objections against his call, Moses had shown his hesitancy to go along with it. As for the people, the recurring motif that they longed for the good days in Egypt, and eventually made plans to return there, fully demonstrated their disagreement with the Lord (Exod. 14:12; 16:3; 17:3; Num. 11:18; 14:2 ff.; 20:3 ff.).

Yet the goal was relentlessly pursued, and in doing so the Lord continuously manifested his strength and power. With his power he both helped and punished. In responding to the "murmurings" with the miracles at Marah, water from the rock, the manna, the quails, and the bronze serpent, he helped; in sending fire and plagues he punished. Yet in acting in the two directions of help and punishment he was at work always to reach his goal, the salvation of his people. By the miracles, he kept them alive; by his punishments, he demonstrated that he did not tolerate human resistance attempting to frustrate his purpose. Even the punishments, therefore, serve the divine saving plan and illustrate an idea common to the entire Old Testament: He who accepts the plan of God shares the fruits of his victories; he who resists faces destruction. The destruction, however, follows only in extreme cases. Only when it was beyond doubt that the rebellious generation was unable to go along with God's plan were they prevented from entering the promised land and had to accept death in the wilderness. But even then the people as such were not destroyed.

The second reason for the Lord's forgiveness is his glory and fame. As the author believes, it is vital that he should demonstrate his superior strength against all opposing forces and that this be made known among all nations (Exod. 7:5; 9:29; 14:17; 32:11 ff.; Num. 14:13, etc.). In seeking his glory, however, the Lord is not selfish. In spreading his fame he also works salvation for his people. According to the author there is a specific divine goal—the Lord's glory and fame—independent from any human purpose and interest, but the good of his people is included in that goal. The glory and fame of the Lord and the good of the people, therefore, always go hand in hand (cf. note 5, ch. 5).

The third reason the Lord is merciful is that he wants to keep Israel in his possession. According to the Old Testament, obedience to the Lord, i.e., to his law, is a sign that those who obey belong to him. Two of the rebellion stories, therefore, speak about the Lord having "proved," i.e., having put the people on trial, to see whether they are obedient. One is the story of Marah, the other the story of the manna (Exod.

15:23-25; 16:13-21). In both there are bits of tradition not mentioned elsewhere. The first interprets the miracle of sweetening, i.e., healing, the bitter water, as a sign that the Lord is capable of being Israel's healer, provided they keep his "statute and ordinance." The other holds that the commandment of the sabbath was given with the gift of the manna. Therefore, the reason why "on the sixth day, when they prepare what they bring in, it will be twice as much as they gather daily," and why "on the seventh day, which is a sabbath, there will be none" (Exod. 16:5, 26), is that the Lord may see whether they keep the sabbath (vss. 27 ff.). In other words, the water of Marah and the manna are acts of grace and help, in order that by obedience the people may have an opportunity to demonstrate their belonging to the Lord. In the stories about the golden calf and the sin with Baal-Peor, we find the same point. According to the first, even though the "LORD sent a plague upon the people," he renewed the covenant; according to the second, after atonement was made by hanging the "chiefs of the people," the fierce anger of the Lord was turned away from Israel (Num. 25:4). In other words, there is punishment, because the Lord's "name is Jealous" (Exod. 34:14), but since he will not release Israel from his possession, there is also forgiveness.

The rebellion stories of cultic personnel (Miriam, Nadab, Abihu, Korah, Dathan and Abiram) demonstrate the same "jealousy" of the Lord. The covenant between him and Israel is based on the revelation through Moses, and reconciliation depends on the service of the priesthood created through him. If these foundations are violated, the communion is threatened. This is why Miriam, even though she was a legitimate prophetess, must yield to her brother, and this is why those who wanted to change the institutions of reconciliation had to die.

It is now possible to summarize briefly the message of the

author of the Tetrateuch in the rebellion stories. It is somewhat as follows:

The Lord had a plan which he had made known to the
patriarchs. That plan was to make their descendants into a
nation of his own, and to give them the land of Canaan. After
many centuries of waiting, now he began to act and realize his
plan. At one time his goal was not set as a response to human
initiative; it was a sovereign decision. But his decision to act
now is a response to Israel's "groaning." In saying this, the
author agreed with the general thrust of the Bible that in the
divine plan man's good is included and the divine acts are
directed for his salvation. Or, to say the same thing in other
words, God is known only as being concerned with man and
acting for him.

In the struggle for the realization of his plan, God met in-
difference, lack of confidence, rejection, even rebellion, both
on the part of the man Moses, whom he had elected for his
representative, and of the people. Yet he never gave up. If
there was no other way, he punished, even destroyed, those
who resisted; but, because the realization of his plan depended
on the existence of the people, he never destroyed them utterly.
Thus one reason for his forgiveness was perseverance in his
plan, in his promise. The other reason for forgiving was that
had he destroyed Israel, his "fame," his reputation, would have
been ruined among the nations. The third reason the Lord
showed grace was that he wanted to keep Israel in his possession. In certain cases, therefore, he gave ordinances, statutes,
or laws, that by obeying them the people might demonstrate
their belonging to him.

While the Lord was gracious, men were rebellious. Moses,
whom he had chosen for his representative, while not against
his plan, gave unfounded excuses to avoid the commission.
Even after he was commanded to accept it, he showed impatience and lack of confidence. Eventually he proved insuffi-

cient to carry out the Lord's plan. In two things, however, he was without fault. First, he never turned to other gods, but remained perfectly faithful. In modern terms this means that he clearly appreciated the essential difference between loyalty to the Lord and fellowship with him, on the one hand, and loyalty to another power and fellowship with it. He fully comprehended that communion with the living God was infinitely more valuable than loyalty to any other values. Second, even at the risk of his life, he voluntarily accepted complete identity with the people to whom he was sent as God's representative. With this he helped the divine plan, paradoxically, against the intention of the Lord himself, who was ready to destroy Israel, on whose existence his plan depended.

The people, however, for whose good God had made his plan and for whose sake Moses resisted the Lord, did not show confidence and loyalty. Many times they doubted that the Lord was strong enough to provide water and food, or that he could give protection against their foes. They also showed an inability to distinguish between the priceless value of belonging to the Lord and their own physical comfort. At times they set delicacies above fellowship with him. They were not bad people; neither were they irreligious. They did not commit any immoral act; neither could they live without religion. But they made no distinction between the Lord and other gods. For them the living God was one of the objects of worship and a possible source of help among others. Many times they also preferred the supposedly comfortable life in Egypt to the Lord. They could not live without values, but the values of the living God and other values were on the same plan, and they chose those that seemed more profitable. In refusing to attack Canaan, eventually they refused to take the final risk in serving the divine plan, and so they were rejected as a generation. But even that could not frustrate the Lord. The children of the rebellious generation were allowed to enter Canaan and abide in the divine communion. God's grace defeated human rebellion.

The rebellions of cultic personnel are of a different kind. With the story of Miriam's rebellion the author proclaims that although legitimate prophecy is valid, it cannot set itself above the authority of revelation through Moses, i.e., above the cultic and legal order established through him. That particular revelation, and the form of life created by it, is supreme, and only within its limits is prophetic activity permissible. The rebellion of Aaron's sons, introducing alien rites, and the rebellion of Korah say the same thing essentially, and more. As the author believed, the Lord established valid means of reconciliation. Deviation from them would challenge the divine will to hold Israel within the Lord's realm and would endanger his plan.

3
THE EMERGENCE OF THE REBELLION MOTIF IN HISTORY

How did this strange and, in the history of religion, unique conviction that Israel continuously rebelled against her God arise? Setting aside until the next chapter the detailed analysis of the questions of why the author incorporated the rebellion stories into his work and what the significance of his teaching was for his contemporaries through them, we shall here search only for the historical reasons. There must have been such reasons. The specific nature of Israel's religion was that all essential beliefs grew out of her encounter with history. The rest of the convictions preached by the Tetrateuch also had some historical truth behind them, or at least they arose because of certain historical circumstances.

The Yahwist created his collection of legends and fragmentary myths in the early beginnings under specific historical circumstances. His aim was to clarify for his generation why Israel was elected from all mankind and was helped to security and blessedness under David and Solomon. The convictions taught by the patriarchal stories (that the land of Canaan belongs to Israel by divine promise, that the Lord loves and protects Israel) had behind them at least the actual historical figures of the ancient fathers who once roamed the land and were loved and protected by the Lord. The stories of the exodus reflected the movements of the seminomadic clans, some of whom came from Egypt, others from Sinai. In the process of growth of tradition through the centuries these ancient stories were expanded, and absorbed many other elements, such as the legal and cultic material; yet tradition could never have assumed its present form had the historical events constituting the center of crystallization never happened. Was the unique conviction about the rebelliousness of Israel without historical roots? Is it possible to detect any real history behind the rebellion stories?

Unfortunately no such roots can be found in detail. The time when the Tetrateuch was in the process of assuming its present form—during and after the captivity—was separated from the actual events by some seven centuries, and the memories of the events were already transformed into traditional stories. The reference to the rebellions in the first half of the Book of the Conquest, Deuteronomy, indicate familiarity with many of them almost in their Tetrateuchal forms (Deut. 1:22 ff.; 4:3; 9:6 ff., 22). This early date (ca. 800 B.C.) shows that most of the stories were fixed in tradition long before the captivity and that actual history had been considerably changed in them.

Some conjectures can be made. It can be conjectured, for example, that the stories about Moses in Egypt reflect actual events. The accounts that his mediation was rejected by one of his Hebrew brothers and that the foremen rebuked him because of unsuccessful intervention with the pharaoh may have preserved the memory that initially he had difficulty in establishing his authority. The information of the P version that he was called in Egypt and that he was refused at first by the people is also probable historically. The murmuring stories may have been a dim recollection that the "rabble" among the people often showed dissatisfaction with the misfortunes of the desert. As is admitted by almost all, the story of the spies reflects the unsuccessful attack of the nomadic clans (later to be part of Israel) from the south against Canaan.[1] The sin with Baal-Peor may testify to the tendency of some Israelites-to-be to worship Canaanite deities even before they reached Canaan.

There are some etiological stories explaining the names of certain places—Mara, Meribah, Kibroth Taavah. Such spots may have really existed and their names may have been connected with more or less real or legendary experiences of the clans in the desert. Of course, the existence of places with such names is no proof for historicity any more than the adoption of known natural phenomena and their exaggeration into miracles are (manna, the quails, water from the rock[2]).

There are rebellion stories which reflect historical facts, but of much later origin. Such are the golden calf, the bronze serpent, and the rebellions of cultic personnel. It has long been recognized that the story of the golden calf is directed against Jeroboam the son of Nebat, who, in order to counteract the influence of Jerusalem upon his subjects, had set up two "golden calves," one in Bethel, the other in Dan, and told his people exactly the same words as Aaron told Israel: "Behold your gods, O Israel, who brought you up out of the land of Egypt" (1 Kings 12:28). The story of the bronze serpent also reflects a later incident. It was told to explain the origin of the bronze serpent worshiped for a long time in the Jerusalem temple. Most probably it was an old Canaanite cultic object, representing the god of healing and fertility. That it was not of Israelite origin is shown by the fact that king Hezekiah eventually broke it into pieces (2 Kings 18:4).

The rebellions of cultic personnel reflect even later events. It has already been mentioned that the story about Miriam's revolt was intended to rebuke interference with cultic matters and that it may have been told against Ezekiel. The story of Nadab and Abihu is of similar nature except that it was directed against two priestly clans who did not agree in all details with the leading priestly circles concerning cultic matters and were, therefore, excluded from the priesthood. There are even traces that the same circles attempted to substitute for them other, non-Aaronic clans, supposedly descendants of Aaron's

uncle, Uzziel (Lev. 10:4 ff.). The combined story of Korah
and of the Reubenites Dathan and Abiram points also to some
post-exilic events. Apparently the clan of Korah claimed
priestly status unsuccessfully. The intention of the priestly
leaders was to exclude them even from the Levitical office; this
time, however, their attempt was frustrated. Even though, according to the story, all of Korah's household were destroyed
(Num. 16:32), the Korahites retained their membership
among the Levites so that, acknowledging the actual state of
things, someone had to insert the note in Numbers 26:11 that
"Notwithstanding, the sons of Korah did not die." And, indeed,
we find abundant evidence in the Chronicler that later the
Korahites were an important Levitical group (1 Chron. 9:19;
26:1, etc.).

That uncertainties concerning priestly rights existed among
the returnees is shown by Ezekiel's plan for the restoration, according to which, as is well known, only the Zadokites would
have been accepted as priests (Ezek. 40:46; 44:15). Even
the loss of genealogical records could have caused confusion
and controversies (Ezra 2:59, 62). If for such reasons people
were excluded from the priesthood or even Israel, they might
have begun a struggle for recognition, and the fact of their
struggle might have been changed into a story from the time of
Israel's beginning. The background of the rebellion of the
Reubenites Dathan and Abiram is very obscure. A possible
conjecture is that before or after the exile a group claiming
Reubenite descent desired leadership in Israel on the grounds
that they were descendants of the oldest son of Jacob. Why
their story was combined with the rebellion of Korah eludes
our knowledge.

These historically possible events, some of which are even
probable, would not, however, have served in themselves as
opportunities for the emergence of a belief in Israel's continual
rebelliousness. The rebellions of cultic personnel certainly
would not do so, because only a particular group opposing the

dominant priestly circles had a part in them, and from what they did no conclusion can be drawn about the rebelliousness of the people as a whole. As a matter of fact, these rebellion stories never became part of generally accepted tradition. The main reason, of course, was that they were post-exilic creations. This is why Deuteronomy knows nothing about them. We are dealing with them because they make the same point as the rest of the rebellion stories, i.e., that no resistance is permitted against God's saving will, and because they make that point in the same form. Yet not even the rest of the rebellion stories, if they are at least partly true, could have given opportunity for the emergence of the conviction of Israel's rebelliousness. During the long time that passed between their actual occurrence and the age of the author, or even of the Book of the Conquest, the rebellions would have been forgotten. After all, no group is pleased to be reminded of the faults of its forefathers. Moses' initial struggles with his people, the dissatisfaction of those whose leader he was, even the pre-conquest worship of Canaanite deities, would have fallen into oblivion. At some point of history something must have happened that forced tradition to remember the events which took place in the time of the exodus and to transform them into stories heavy with the charge of disloyalty against the Lord.

When can we find this point in Israel's history? Or, to put the question in a more concrete form, when did Israel become conscious of the gravity of disloyalty against the Lord? The time of the exodus, the wilderness wanderings, and the conquest cannot come into consideration. This was a time when there was no Israel as yet, and when the nomadic clans, out of which the nation was formed later, were not strict Yahweh worshipers. Unfortunately, we have no reliable sources concerning the "religion of Moses." The Tetrateuch and the introductory part of the Deuteronomic History, the Book of the Conquest, cannot be trusted historically. As is generally admitted, the story in the Tetrateuch is full of exaggerations and both parts of the Book of the Conquest, with their theory that Joshua destroyed all Canaanites, are not reliable. While it cannot be denied that both Moses and Joshua knew the Lord, Joshua 24:14 ff. shows beyond doubt that not all Israelites worshiped the Lord alone.

In surveying the more reliable material available to us, we must agree with those who say that the conquest of Canaan by Israel was by no means a war between the religions of the Israelites and Canaanites but a struggle between invading semi-nomads and the settled population.[3] The incoming Israelites believed, no doubt, that they fought their battles with the help of the Lord, yet they were not absolute monotheists aiming to destroy all other forms of religion. On the contrary, following the practice of the age and if it seemed appropriate, they were ready to enlist among their helpers the deities of the land.

From a much later period we find a striking instance of such an attitude in 2 Kings 1. The story is part of a collection of legends about Elijah but the basic elements are historical. It tells that upon becoming sick, Ahaziah, the son of Ahab, sent to Baal-zebub, the god of Ekron, to inquire "whether I shall recover from this sickness" and, probably, to ask for help. Such "limping with two different opinions" (1 Kings 18:21) must have been even more frequent in earlier times. In rebuking Baalism, the book of Judges, indeed, admits that the baals were worshiped by Israel.

> And the people of Israel did what was evil in the sight of the LORD and served the Baals; and they forsook the LORD, the God of their fathers, who had brought them out of the land of Egypt; they went after other gods, from among the gods of the peoples who were round about them, and bowed down to them; and they provoked the LORD to anger. They forsook the LORD, and served the Baals and the Ashtaroth (Judg. 2:11-13).

As has often been pointed out, the same book views the early history of Israel as a series of such idolatries for which the Lord punished the people over and over again, whereupon

they turned to him and were delivered by judges raised by the
Lord. We even hear that they once accepted Baal-berith for
their god (Judg. 8:33). The long Deuteronomistic sermon in
Judges 2:11 ff. illustrates very well what was going on in those
days when "there was no king in Israel; every man did what
was right in his own eyes" (Judg. 17:6; 21:25). The situation
must have been that the large majority of the Israelites without any feeling of uneasiness acknowledged the baals, the local
manifestations of the great Canaanite god, Baal. As we know
from archeological evidence,[4] Baal was the personification of
fertility in the soil, in man and beast, and as so many fertility
gods and goddesses of the ancient Near East, he was believed
to die every year when the dry season began and was resurrected when the rains arrived again.

The local baals were his manifestations, and to many, if
not to most, Israelite farmers it appeared a necessity to seek
their favor. They admitted that the Lord was the national God
of Israel and he was the God of the wars of Israel, yet because
he was a newcomer in the land, he was of little use when it
came to bringing about a good harvest, an abundance of calves
and lambs, and a great number of children. According to
ancient belief, for such things the ancient gods, at home in the
land, were competent. The Israelite women concurred with this
idea in treasuring statuettes of the fertility goddess in their
homes[5] and in worshiping the queen of heaven (Jer. 44:17).
From a later age, after the Lord became domiciled and it was
believed that the land belonged to him alone, we have a good
illustration of the belief. In 2 Kings 17:24 ff. we read that the
colonists settled in the conquered territory of Northern Israel
asked the Assyrian king to send one of the priests who had
been carried away, because lions had killed many of them.
Their request was granted, the priest was sent, and he "taught
them how they should fear [i.e., worship] the LORD" (vs. 28).

This being the case, it is no wonder that there are many

traces of baal worship during the period of judges, the time
when the Israelite tribes lived in the loose organization of the
tribal confederacy whose only binding force was the common
sanctuary of the ark and the yearly national festivals at the
place where the ark happened to be.[6] Such syncretism between
Yahwism and baalism is demonstrated by the story of Gideon
(Judg. 6-9). Perhaps that part of the story which tells of
Gideon destroying the altar of Baal is a later addition, yet the
memory that the Israelites erected such altars was correct.
The original name of Gideon, Jerubbaal (Judg. 7:1; 8:29;
9:1, etc.)—which is piously explained by the author (Judg.
6:32)—shows that his father was not reluctant to give a name
to his son which had the name of the Canaanite god in it. In
later times, under Saul, David, Solomon, and other early kings,
both northern and Judean, we find no objection to baal worship. Saul's son and successor was called Ishbaal (or Eshbaal,
1 Chron. 8:33), Man of Baal, changed by the author (or
someone who could not believe it) to Ish-bosheth, Man of
Shame (2 Sam. 2:8). Even David had a son with a theophoric
name of Baal (Beeliada, 1 Chron. 14:7, changed in 2 Sam.
5:16 to Eliada).

Many other illustrations could be mentioned which would
show that Baal was not hated by the Israelites in early times.
Anyone who wishes more evidence can find it in surveying the
list of individual and geographical names containing the name
of Baal in a concordance. If this is the case in the present text,
which was carefully edited to avoid any appearance of approv-
ing baalism, then in other forms of tradition, rejected by the
authors, there must have been many other instances.

We have other, mostly non-biblical, evidence that Canaanite culture, of which religion was a part, influenced Israel
strongly. The influence can be detected in all ways of life, first
of all religion itself. As is well known, Solomon's temple was
built by Canaanites (Phoenicians) and after Canaanite pat-

tern. In Canaanite documents, found at Ugarit, parallels can be found to the cultic function of the Israelite king, the organization of the priesthood, the sacrificial system, social institutions, and to some extent, even to the idea of the divine.[7] It is probable that a large body of law, now in the so-called Book of the Covenant (Exod. 21-23), was borrowed from the Canaanites.[8] Even some Psalms have been adopted from the Canaanite cult but, of course, with adequate changes to fit the worship of the Lord.[9] Indeed, during the age of the confederacy and the early centuries of the monarchy, the culture of Canaan had conquered Israel. The tribes adapted themselves well—indeed, too well—to their new homeland. No, that time could not give rise to the conviction that Israel was disloyal to the Lord. It was a time of syncretism with baalism rather than an encounter with it. Of course, it is possible, even probable, that in those early days there were people who fought for the exclusive worship of the Lord in Israel. They should be sought among the prophets and, perhaps, such people who were both prophetic individuals and leading national figures as Samuel or David. For the time being, however, their efforts were not crowned with success.

From all this it may be concluded that we have to search for another period of Israel's history when a conflict between baalism and Yahwism took place, a conflict which made Baal and baalism abominable, if not in the eyes of all, at least in the eyes of the religious leaders. When can we find such a period? Two periods come under consideration: the period of the Omrides and that of the great Mesopotamian empires.

The conflict, however, did not occur in Judah first. There we find that Canaanite and other originally non-Judean groups existed peacefully together. Some of these groups may even have joined Judah, either by becoming one of its clans, or, perhaps, as members of a possible six-tribe southern confederacy. Such groups were the Calebites, Othnielites, Kenites,

Jerahmeelites, and Kenizzites (Num. 24:21; 32:12; Joshua 14:6 ff.; 15:15 ff.; Judg. 4:11; 1 Sam. 15:6; 30:29). The lack of aversion is shown also by the fact that David, in occupying Jerusalem, did not exterminate the inhabitants, the Jebusites, but had a friendly relationship with them even though their god was not the Lord (2 Sam. 24:18-23). It seems, therefore, that the absorption of the Canaanite element was gradual and by and large peaceful in Judah.

The story was different in the Northern Kingdom. There we find, indeed, a period, sufficiently attested to by biblical evidence, when a conflict arose between Yahwism and baalism. It ended with the defeat of the latter, and the encounter gave the opportunity to remember the old rebellions of Israel.

The period was that of the dynasty of Omri. His image and the image of his son Ahab are unsympathetically portrayed in the Deuteronomic History. But judging not from a convictional, religious viewpoint, both were among the greatest rulers of the North. The Bible informs us that Omri was the commander-in-chief of the Israelite army when he revolted against the usurping king, Zimri, forced him to commit suicide, and after defeating an opponent, Tibni, occupied the throne. Whether he was appointed "by the Lord," i.e., by some prophet, as was usually required for all northern kings, we do not know (1 Kings 16:15 ff.). At any rate, he became a powerful ruler, and was also well known internationally, so much so that even Jehu (who overthrew his dynasty) was called the "son of Omri" by the Assyrian king, Shalmaneser III, on his famous black obelisk. Omri's son, Ahab, was not less significant. He participated with two thousand chariots and ten thousand foot soldiers in a campaign against the same Assyrian king, a fact recorded by Shalmaneser himself.[10]

During the whole period of the Omrides, there was a bitter struggle with the Arameans of Damascus, in which, even though the Israelites proved in general the weaker, they were able to preserve independence. They also established favorable international relations, especially with the two Phoenician-Canaanite cities Sidon and Tyre. In spite of their successful reign, however, Omri and Ahab made a mistake which was unforgivable in the sight of the ardent Yahwists, probably people who still cherished the ideas of the confederacy: They favored, or at least did not resist, baalism in their own realm and supported it also in Judah. We are not familiar with the details, but biblical evidence indicates that under the Omrides, with the exception of the last member of the dynasty, Jehoram, Yahwism was threatened mortally.

This is what we are able to collect from the biblical record: Six years after he ascended the throne, Omri changed the capital of the Northern Kingdom from Tirzah to Samaria, which in ancient times meant change of policy (1 Kings 16:24).[11] The Bible acknowledges that he had shown might, but condemns him bitterly (1 Kings 16:25-28). He was followed by Ahab who, apparently still during the lifetime of his father, had married Jezebel, the daughter of Ethbaal king of the Sidonians, who, according to non-biblical sources, resided in Tyre and was the leading ruler of the Phoenicians.[12] This, of course, meant political alliance between the two nations. Ahab "erected an altar for Baal in the house [i.e., temple] of Baal, which he built in Samaria" (1 Kings 16:32); he also built an Asherah, i.e., a pillar consecrated to the fertility goddess, and set up another pillar, apparently in the royal Yahweh sanctuary (later removed by his son, Jehoram, 2 Kings 3:2). He is strongly condemned by the Deuteronomic author. "Ahab did more to provoke the LORD, the God of Israel, to anger than all the kings of Israel who were before him" (vs. 33). His daughter (or sister? 2 Kings 8:18, 26) Athaliah was married to Jehoram of Judah, and a Baal temple was also built in Jerusalem (2 Kings 11:18). Thus baalism was officially recognized in both capitals of Israel.

But the faithful Yahwists reacted vehemently. In 1 Kings 17-19—a story taken from an ancient source dealing with the acts of the prophets Elijah and Elisha but which has historical truth in it—we are informed to some extent about what happened. A leader of the prophetic group, Elijah, most probably supported by the depositories of the confederate tradition, began a relentless struggle against baalism. First he succeeded in restoring the cult of the Lord on Mount Carmel—probably originally a Baal sanctuary—and then with the help of the people of the land, and with the reluctant assistance of Ahab, had the personnel of the Baal cult massacred. Thereupon Jezebel the queen took measures against the extreme wing of the Yahwists, had a number of prophets killed, and also tried to liquidate Elijah. Remarkably, Ahab remained neutral, an onlooker of the struggle, and so did the greater part of the people.

Of course, Yahwism was not outlawed, but baalism became something like a second religion and gained prestige. From the word of the Lord in 1 Kings 19:15-18 we can conclude that the Yahwists did not give up. They conspired to overthrow the dynasty of Omri by setting up Jehu as king (1 Kings 19:16). The details are not known, but evidently nothing could be done during Ahab's reign and the lifetime of Elijah. About fifteen years had to pass (1 Kings 22:51; 2 Kings 8:25 ff.) before their plans could be realized. At this time, under King Joram, the second son of Ahab, the Yahwists made their move. We are informed reliably by 2 Kings 9 about the events. A prophet came to Jehu, apparently the commander-in-chief of the army engaged in war against the Syrians, and anointed him king with the commission to overthrow the last of the Omrides, Joram. The plot must have been known to the rest of the military leaders, because as soon as Jehu told what happened, he was immediately hailed as king (vs. 13). With the consent of the army, Jehu then proceeded to take hold of the kingship. At this time Joram was recuperating from his wounds at the royal estate in Jezreel where the Judean king, Ahaziah, was visiting him. Thus Jehu, who immediately after being anointed rode to Jezreel, was able first to kill Joram and then to mortally wound Ahaziah. The latter fled to a Canaanite city, Megiddo, and died there (vss. 24, 27 ff.).

Having seized the kingship, Jehu proceeded to exterminate baalism. First he had Jezebel, now the queen mother, thrown out the window of the royal residence; then, in order to relieve himself of responsibility, he had all Omrides killed at the hands of the royal officers themselves, and liquidated their party (2 Kings 10:1-11). Initially, his revolt must have appeared to all as one of the dynastic struggles so frequent in the Northern Kingdom, so that not even the leaders of baalism were suspicious. Thus Jehu could play the part of an ardent worshiper of Baal, call a solemn assembly for the god, gathering all the leaders together. At this occasion he himself offered the sacrifice in the Baal temple, after which he had all the cultic personnel destroyed by the royal guard. "Thus Jehu wiped out Baal from Israel" (2 Kings 10:18-28).

These events did not remain without consequences in Judah. When queen Athaliah heard that her son, Ahaziah, was assassinated, she attempted to do the same thing to the dynasty of David that Jehu had done to the Omrides; she had all male members of David's descendants killed,[13] except one infant child, Joash, who was stolen away by Jehosheba, the sister of Ahaziah (probably not a daughter of Athaliah) and wife of Jehoiada, the chief priest of Jerusalem. The child was kept in the temple area and raised secretly. Athaliah, apparently having killed her own grandsons too, became queen of the realm, the only one in Israel's history, and usurped the throne for seven years. After this time the chief priest organized a palace revolt, and with the consent of the "people of the land" and with the assistance of the royal guard, made the child Joash king. During the coronation ceremony Athaliah was killed, the

Baal temple erected by her razed, and the chief priest of Baal also killed. This put an end to baalism in Judah, too (2 Kings 11).

What did all this mean? The general scholarly opinion is that the Omrides did not pose any serious threat to Yahwism. It is believed that the erection of the Baal temple in Samaria was nothing more than the usual courtesy extended to foreign queens, a practice also followed by Solomon (1 Kings 11:1-8). Even scholars who have a keen eye in evaluating the sources believe this.[14] Yet there are indications in the extant material, and the known political situation suggests, that under the Omrides an attempt was made by the Canaanite elements, still found in the land, to restore their supremacy in Palestine.

Under the Omrides such an attempt promised success. In the first place, after the division of the Davidic-Solomonic realm the political influence of the Canaanites increased in the North, because the proportion of the Canaanites to the Israelites shifted in favor of the Canaanites. Under David and Solomon, in the united realm, the proportion of the Canaanites to the Israelites was not too large, being balanced by the Judean population. But when after Solomon the large Canaanite cities in the northwestern corner of the land fell to the Northern Kingdom, the situation changed and the proportion of the Canaanites increased. Besides, these cities immediately adjoined the territories of Sidon and Tyre. Because of the Aramean threat, the Omrides had to be on good terms with the Phoenicians and had to make concessions to them. In the cultural atmosphere of the age this meant not only political but also religious concessions. One indication of this is that at the ancient Baal sanctuary on Mount Carmel, the altar of the Lord, built probably under David or Solomon to signify Israelite supremacy,[15] was thrown down and had to be repaired by Elijah (1 Kings 18:30). All this undoubtedly strengthened the importance of the Canaanites within the Israelite realm.

The usual objection that the Omrides permitted the cult of the great Phoenician god, Baal Melkart, and that his cult was different from the cult of the baals, the local numina of fertility, loses credence if we consider that the cultures of the Phoenicians and the Canaanites were very close to each other and therefore in practice there was little difference between their religions. For the average man it was unnoticeable. Besides, as was indicated, at this time all realms of Israelite life were deeply saturated with Canaanite influence, so much so that even if it was believed that the Lord was the fount of all blessings and help, his function was very similar to the function of Baal Melkart and the baals.

In the biblical record we find traces that a shift was taking place from Yahwism to baalism. Omri is of unknown origin; his name and the name of Ahab are not Israelite. He had changed the capital of the land, and this may indicate that he was turning away from the old Israelite values. His family apparently had a private residence in Canaanite territory, on the plain of Jezreel.[16] Joram went there to recuperate from his wounds, he entertained Ahaziah there, and Jezebel was sojourning in the city of Jezreel when Jehu had her killed. This area was subdued first by Jehu; here was the stronghold of Ahab's "great men, and his familiar friends, and his priests" (2 Kings 9:30 ff.; 10:11), whom Jehu killed. All this indicates that the Omrides relied politically on the Canaanites rather than on the Israelites. It is also to be noted that Ahaziah, being mortally wounded, fled to a Canaanite city, probably because he did not trust the Israelites. The Baal worshipers felt very secure at this time; they saw no threat in Jehu's revolt against their religion. When Jehu issued a proclamation that "Ahab served Baal a little; but Jehu will serve him much," everyone believed it, and at his invitation all leaders of baalism came without being suspicious.

The most important, and as far as the present writer can

see, decisive evidence that the Canaanites planned a mortal blow to everything that was truly Israelite is the case of Athaliah. By birth she was not a foreign queen to whom a courtesy had to be extended to practice her religion; yet she had built a Baal temple in Jerusalem. After Jehu's revolt she attempted to annihilate the strongest support of Yahwism, the Davidic dynasty, and seized the kingdom herself. All this is not understandable without assuming that her ultimate aim was to exterminate Yahwism. It is also characteristic that Jehoiada's revolt was wholeheartedly supported by the doubtless strongly Yahwistic "people of the land."

This was, therefore, the time when Israel became sharply conscious of her specific heritage. Perhaps it was the first time in her history that a clear distinction was made between the Lord and an alien god, Baal. At this time the zealous adherents of the Lord realized the gravity of disloyalty to him. Before or shortly after the revolt of Jehu, I believe, a work was produced by those who supported him with the aim of giving a program for the reorganization of pure Yahwism and for the elimination of baalism. This was the Book of the Conquest (Deut.-Joshua 11). At this time the rebellions of Israel, already part of tradition, came into sharp focus, as can be seen in the original introduction to the work (Deut. 9:6-24), and served as a motif to frighten Israel and keep her from committing the sin of disloyalty again. From this time on, nothing was consciously accepted from the Canaanites, and worship of any god besides the Lord was rebuked vehemently, at least by those who stayed within the mainstream of Israel's religion. From a period only eighty-odd years later than Jehu, we possess the first prophetic utterances, those of Hosea, Amos, Isaiah, and Micah, who fought either explicitly against baalism or against Canaanite practices in the cult and in the way of life of the Israelites. Of course we can assume with certainty that these voices represented the minority, and both the worship of the baals and further syncretism with baalism went on practically undisturbed. Even in such late prophetic utterances as those of Jeremiah, preserved in the collection under his name, the struggle against the baals goes on. But from now on all this met strong opposition.

The second period during which Israel became conscious of her heritage and the sinfulness of disloyalty to the Lord was the age of the great Mesopotamian empires, from the middle of the eighth century until the fall of Jerusalem in 587. As is well known, these empires, first Assyria, then Babylonia, subdued the small states of Syria-Palestine, either conquering them outright or making them vassals. In ancient times conquest meant not only political submission but also recognition that the conqueror's gods were superior to those of the conquered (1 Kings 20:23). Thus, as far as religious affairs were concerned, the vassal had to accept and worship the gods of the overlord.[17]

We have no biblical record of what happened in Samaria before it fell in 722. For example, we do not know if Jehu, who according to non-biblical sources was a vassal to Assyria, worshiped its gods, but of Judah we know positively that in Jerusalem the cult of Assyrian gods was introduced. Seeking protection from Tiglath-pileser III against Israel and Damascus, Ahaz, king of Judah, submitted voluntarily to Assyrian suzerainty. Having become a vassal, he had to accept the Assyrian gods. In 2 Kings 16 we read that even before returning from the audience with Tiglath-pileser, Ahaz ordered changes in the Jerusalem cult, had a new altar made, and closed the royal entrance to the temple, thus probably acknowledging that the Assyrian king and not he had sovereign rights in the temple. Such a step helped not only the revival of Canaanitism but also a syncretism, now with the religion of Mesopotamia. Ahaz's son, Hezekiah, in breaking with Assyria put an end not only to baalism but also to the worship of the Assyrian gods (2

Kings 18:4 ff.). But his son Manasseh opened the dam before the flood. In 2 Kings 21 we have the disappointing report about the worship of both Canaanite and Mesopotamian gods.

The reform of Josiah, the grandson of Manasseh, was concerned not only with the destruction of the local Israelite sanctuaries—where no doubt much of Canaanitism was practiced—but also with the elimination of Assyrian religion (2 Kings 23:11 ff.). From prophetic utterances, preserved in extant prophetic collections, we also find ample evidence about the worship of Mesopotamian deities in Jerusalem.[18] It is very probable that the "evil kings," Ahaz and Manasseh, introduced the worship of Assyrian deities against their better judgment, and if they could, would have rejected them. But rejection would have meant eventual disaster. For prophets, however, like Isaiah, Micah, Zephaniah, and Jeremiah, this was no excuse. They were too deeply conditioned by the zealous spirit of Yahwism born at the time of the Omrides, Elijah, Jehu, and the Book of the Conquest; against all sound political principles of the age, they insisted on the exclusive worship of the Lord and on trust in him alone. No doubt they had many followers. Much of the "innocent blood" with which Manasseh "had filled Jerusalem from one end to another" (2 Kings 21:16) was the blood of those who resisted his religious policy.

During this period the difference between the Lord and other gods became even clearer, and as a result of the prophets' inability to stop the worship of alien gods, the belief in the rebelliousness of Israel was reinforced. Isaiah, with his famous doctrine about the inviolability of Zion (7-8; 14:32; 29:7; 30:15 ff.; 27:2 ff., etc.), played upon the same motif as did the murmuring stories and the stories questioning the Lord's help against Israel's enemies during the exodus: unconditional trust in the Lord. Jeremiah, Micah, and Zephaniah, in condemning all forms of worship of the gods of Assyria, also relied on the tradition of the rebellion stories. For them, and after them for the author of the Deuteronomic History, the worship of Baal—something not necessitated by the political circumstances—and the worship of the sun, of the queen of heaven, and of the hosts of heaven—demanded by the political situation—was of the same nature (2 Kings 23:4-14; Jer. 11: 6-13; 19:4 ff.). But their struggle was in vain. The religious syncretism continued until the fall of Jerusalem (Jer. 44:15 ff.).

Jeremiah and Ezekiel saw no hope for improvement. Jeremiah speaks for all those who believed in the utter corruption of Israel:

> Can the Ethiopian change his skin
>   or the leopard his spots?
> Then also you can do good
>   who are accustomed to do evil (Jer. 13:23; cf. Ezek. 23).

The belief emerged that only divine intervention could save Israel in re-creating her in a manner so that she would be capable of obedience:

> I will sprinkle clean water upon you, and you shall be clean from all your uncleannesses, and from all your idols I will cleanse you. A new heart I will give you, and a new spirit I will put within you; and I will take out of your flesh the heart of stone and give you a heart of flesh. And I will put my spirit within you, and cause you to walk in my statutes and be careful to observe my ordinances (Ezek. 36:25-27; cf. Jer. 31:31 ff.).

The new heart and the new spirit were not given in the same way Ezekiel had hoped; neither was the new covenant made after the manner of Jeremiah. But first the Deuteronomic History, relying on the tradition of the Book of the Conquest, then the Tetrateuch, and finally, after the captivity, the Chronicler, made use of the motif of Israel's rebelliousness. All three pointed out the horrible sin of idolatry both in the form of baalism and in the form of worship of Mesopotamian deities. The prophetic utterances made in the heat of the struggle before the exile were collected and edited for the purpose of teaching Israel not to commit this sin any more. Along with other convictions equally necessary for Israel's restoration, the stories of the rebellions became part of the synagogal instruction. And then, in a sense, the hopes of Jeremiah and Ezekiel were fulfilled. Even though restored Israel never became faultless, in one respect she became perfect: After Ezra and Nehemiah, idolatory never again became a problem for the mainstream of Judaism. The Maccabean revolt and the survival of Judaism, with its pure monotheism and perfect trust in the Lord, cannot be imagined without the conviction behind the motif of Israel's rebelliousness, which negatively yet forcefully declared: There is no God but the Lord and all help comes from him.

4
THE MEANING
OF THE REBELLION MOTIF

The second part of the Tetrateuch, which contains the story of the deliverance from Egypt, the establishment of the covenant at Sinai, and the wanderings in the wilderness, begins with an astounding piece of information:

> Then Joseph died, and all his brothers, and all that generation. But the descendants of Israel were fruitful and increased greatly; they multiplied and grew exceedingly strong; so that the land was filled with them (Exod. 1:6-7).

The information is astounding because, according to P, "the time that the people of Israel dwelt in Egypt was four hundred and thirty years" (Exod. 12:40; Gen. 15:13). This was the number of years that passed between the arrival of Jacob in Egypt and the rise of the new king who did not know Joseph; that is, this brief remark covers the history of more than four centuries. As against this historical summary told in two short sentences, in his work, now divided into four books, the author devoted the material now comprising the books of Exodus, Leviticus, and Numbers to the history of the forty years spent by Israel in the wilderness. Whatever one might think of the actual chronology—and we have very little information about that—this situation shows the nature of the author's history writing.

For a modern writer of history to summarize the events of more than four centuries in one sentence and then devote a long story to one-tenth of that period would be an unforgivable mistake. But this should not be surprising for those who are familiar with the nature of biblical history writing. In the Bible only events are told in which, as the writer believed, God did something significant. This was also the method of our author, except that he had a specific reason for writing at length about the forty years. What was the reason?

In order to understand him, we have to go back to an idea well known to all forms of religion, the idea of the *archetype*. As students of comparative religion inform us, for religion in general and particularly for primitive religion, no act was meaningful unless it was the repetition of an act performed "once upon a time," at the beginning of all things. As a rule it was believed that these acts were done not by ordinary human beings but by gods or almost-divine culture heroes.[1] There are a great number of examples for this archetypal thinking. We find culture heroes in China, represented by the mythical emperors, among the Indians of both Americas and of northern Asia, and in Australia.[2] The same pattern appears in all cases: Once upon a time when humanity still lived under barbarous conditions, either the creator god, some other gods, or mythical humans appeared who taught all elements of culture and the details of civilization based on that culture; they taught how to produce silk, pursue agriculture, build houses, etc. The same divine or semi-divine personages also established religious rites. Whatever they taught or established had to be repeated accurately, without any change. If this was done, life had meaning, the harvest was bountiful, the group lived in peace, and the cultic rites were effective. If this was not done, chaos and disaster threatened.

The same archetypal cultures, whether on a primitive or higher stage, also ascribed great significance to the myth. For them the myth was not a made-up, untrue story as it is for us. It was an event which took place in the primeval age, an event whose actors were divine, which initiated either the ordered world or effected a basic change in the already existing order. The belief, then, was that by the recitation or reenactment of the primordial event the same effective power was released as by the original, archetypal act, and the existing cosmic order was reinforced and secured. Thus, if the myth of creation was recited or reenacted by significant personages—king, priest, or priestess—the cosmos was rejuvenated, the soil was made capable of producing the same abundance of food, men and beasts were made as fertile as in the primeval time.[3] The mythological event could also change the existing order. Up until the time Persephone was snatched away to the underworld and subsequently restored to her mother for part of the year, there was eternal summer; since that time there has been a succession of seasons. There is a large body of material collected by students of comparative religion for the illustration of archetypal thinking, but this is not the place to mention it in detail. A few instances to clarify the nature of the Tetrateuchal author's teaching and preaching will suffice.

One example is from a culture with which Israel had no contact at all. We are informed about a ritual in ancient India which had the intent of recovering the cosmos from the Titans and securing it to the gods of order. The myth of the ritual tells that at one time the Titans defeated the gods in all quarters of the cosmos except one, the northeastern. In order to recover the lost quarters, they elected one of their number, Soma, as king, and he accomplished the task. According to the Indian myth, Soma was both a god, a plant, and a drink made of that plant, and personified the life-force of vegetation. Since the cosmos was reconquered by him in the mythical time, his act had to be repeated in order to strengthen vegetation. A priest, therefore, took the place of Soma and repeated his successful conquest. He put the Soma drink on a cart and, as in the archetypal time, carried it around to all quarters of the sacred area, representing the cosmos, and thereby brought about the same effect, compelling the forces of nature to produce abundant food.[4]

Another example is from the geographical area of Israel, from her powerful neighbor Egypt. The idea does not refer to a mythical event but to an archetypal, primordial force, *Maat,* personified as the goddess of wisdom. In a paradoxical, alogical manner, so typical of ancient Egypt, she was the daughter of Re (or Atum, both creator gods), and at the same time the eye of her father, the eye which gave him power and divine nature. According to the myth, Maat, as the personification of the force in the cosmic order, was produced with the act of creation. As Morenz defines the idea, this force was responsible for the "correct order of all things in nature and society, established in the creative act, and now it represents that which is correct and proper, it represents the law, order, justice and truth."[5] Having descended from heaven in the mythical time, the good order created by her has to be maintained forever, and if violated must be restored to its archetypal validity by the divine king, the pharaoh. It is law, but not statutory; it is a basic value (*Grundwert*) to which all acts have to comply. He who follows it is filled with magical power and receives eternal life. Students of religion will easily recognize the similarity of Maat with the Indian *Rta*, the Chinese *Tao*, the Confucian *Li*, and the Hebrew *chokma*, and will also see that it is a specific version of the all-pervading force which, according to the overwhelming majority of religions, gives unity and true life to all corporate bodies.

The third example is, again, the repetition of an archetypal myth. It is also taken from the cultural area of which Israel was a part, Mesopotamia. It is the famed New Year festival (the *akitu* festival) well known to biblical scholars. Although not all the details are available, what is known is sufficient to understand the meaning. The festival was celebrated in the same form from the time of the Sumerians, and was adopted later by Babylonians and Assyrians. Its ritual was something like the following: On the first day of the month

Nisan, in the spring, the chief priest, after due preparations and purifications, recited the creation myth which told about the fight between the creator god—in Babylon, Marduk—and the personification of chaos, Tiamat. Although the text of the creation myth does not mention it,[6] the recitation also had a passage which said that Marduk was first slain, and not until after his revival did he win the victory. This is, apparently, a Tammuz motif, from a vegetation myth, according to which Tammuz, the lover of the vegetation goddess, Ishtar, died and was later revived by the goddess.

During the time Marduk was dead, the king was taken to the shrine of Marduk where the chief priest stripped him of his regalia, slapped at his face, forced him to kneel, and pulled his ears. The king then recited a negative confession declaring that he did not do anything that might have harmed the city of Babylon. Thereupon the king rose, received his regalia back, and then was slapped again at his cheek to produce tears from his eyes. If this happened, it was a good omen for the New Year. During the humiliation of the king there was commotion on the streets and mock battles were fought, apparently repeating the fight of Marduk with Tiamat. After this the gods, i.e., their statues, were taken to the festival house on the outskirts of the city in a procession on the sacred way. There a banquet was arranged for the gods, the king, and the participants. At some point, the sacred marriage union took place between the king and the queen or the king and a priestess of high rank. In conclusion, the gods determined the destiny of the New Year, whereupon they were returned to their respective temples.[7]

If we accept that the recitation and the reenactment of the myth meant the restoration of the primeval time and released the primeval energy, the festival is not difficult to interpret, and, indeed, is done in about the same manner by all scholars. The Tammuz motif appears three times: once in that passage of the recitation according to which Marduk died and was revived; second, in the humiliation and the reinstallation of the king playing the part of the god, which stands for the god's death and resurrection; and third, in the sacred marriage of the king with the queen or priestess. The death of Marduk and the humiliation of the king symbolize the death of vegetation, while the revival of Marduk and the reinstallation of the king not only symbolize, but, by the repetition of the mythical event, also release the primeval energy, help to bring about the renewal of fertility, and secure the abundance of vegetation and harvest. The sacred marriage, by impregnating the female, has the same effect—it brings fertility to nature. The recitation of the creation myth and the mock battles reenact the creation of order from chaos and, as other mythical repetitions, rejuvenate the cosmos.

What has all this to do with our problem, the story in the Tetrateuch and the rebellions of Israel? On the surface, little, perhaps nothing, but at closer inspection a basic similarity appears. As the Indian ritual, the idea of Maat, and the myths recited and reenacted in Babylon were archetypal, so are the institutions ordered during the forty years. We find that in his whole work, one of the important methods of the author for proclaiming his convictions and giving weight to his ordinances was the idea of the archetype. In a way, the patriarchal stories were also archetypal. The patriarchs, as roots, foreshadowed the destiny of Israel. The story holds that whatever happened to the patriarchs will happen to Israel. As they were chosen by the Lord, as they were protected, were at home in the land, so will Israel be chosen, be protected, be at home in the land, and will lead a happy life. The story of the forty years, however, is archetypal in a different way. It deals with the people descended from the roots, the patriarchs, and in their lifetime the promises prefigured by the story of the patriarchs are now fulfilled. Only some of the exodus stories are archetypal in the same way as the patriarchal stories, as the fight with the pharaoh or the motifs of the manna, the quails, and water from the rock. These also hold the promise that Israel will be helped. In the rest of the stories, however, since the promises prefigured in the life of the roots have been fulfilled, not the promises are important but the creation of those institutions which keep the people in the Lord's fellowship. Such archetypal institutions are the law, the figures of Moses and Aaron, and the cult.[8]

The law, in creating a design of life to be followed forever, is archetypal. In Israel there was no way of making new laws either by royal decree or by some parliamentary procedure. The law, given in the archetypal time, was unchangeable. If at a later time but still before the canonization of the Torah there was need for a new law, it was enacted by projecting a theoretical precedent to the archetypal age, e.g., the law about the inheritance of girls without brothers, for which the archetypal precedent of the daughters of Zelophehad was created (Num. 27:1 ff.; 36). How deeply rooted the idea of the archetypal law was is shown by the fact that the talmudic rabbis never thought that they created new laws; they believed that they only interpreted the old ones.

In considering the two most prominent personages in the Tetrateuch, Moses and Aaron, there is some difficulty with the figure of Moses as an archetype. As has been mentioned, he is a kingly figure, and yet the Tetrateuch never speaks about the monarchy. Was the author's intention, perhaps, to preach that this institution, even in the form of the Davidic dynasty, was against the will of the Lord? In this case, of course, Moses would not be an archetype but rather a warning against setting up anything like a kingship, because there was only one royal figure in Israel, and that was Moses, whose unique role could never be repeated. Or was the intention of the author to state exactly the contrary, i.e., that the kings of Israel should look upon Moses as an ideal? Evidence seems to point toward the first alternative. As has been noticed by scholars, in the post-exilic community the high priest took the place and performed the function of the king. The careful and detailed description of Aaron's vestment in Exodus 28 and 39, as well as his solemn consecration in Exodus 29 and Leviticus 8, suggests royal dignity. At any rate, unlike Moses, Aaron is a true archetype. He is the first high priest; therefore, all his successors must wear the same vestment, have to be consecrated exactly in the same manner, and perform the functions as he did.

The lengthy descriptions of cultic acts, sacrifices, consecratory and purificatory rites, and the feasts are also archetypal. They must be performed unchanged forever (Lev. 6:18; 16: 29; 23:14, 41, etc.). The similarity between the belief expressed in the Tetrateuch concerning the origin of the rites and the archetypal thinking of non-biblical religions is striking. One might almost say that during the forty years, the Lord acted as the high gods or culture heroes acted for the primitives. All important institutions upon which the life of Israel depended were established at this time. The idea never changed. After the destruction of the temple, when the rabbis of the Talmud recorded the cult in hairsplitting detail,[9] they did it in loyalty to the principle: This is the way things have been done always, since the time of Moses, and thus it has to be done when the temple will be built up again, forever.

Yet in spite of a basic similarity there are important differences. The archetypal period functions as the mythical period of other religions, but it is not of the same nature; it does not create culture and civilization in the proper sense of the word; the design of life, the law, does not flow from a "basic value" granted to man; there is no release of primeval energy by the repetition of mythical acts, and neither are the cultic rites effective by mere repetition.

The archetypal period functions as a myth, but it is not of

the same nature as in other religions. In other religions the myth is an event which makes history possible, but strictly speaking, it does not take place in history. As a divine act, it is the reason that human life exists in its present form. It is the foundation upon which all things are built. In Mesopotamia, after the gods were born, it was decided to create men in order to have slaves to feed the gods. Because of this divine decision, historical humanity is a mass of slaves serving their superhuman lords, and the king is the chief of the slaves, a tenant farmer of the gods, who is called to account every year.[10] In Egypt, Ptah brought the gods into existence, created order in chaos, initiated farming, and established the social order. The structures of society and civilization in the present time, in history, therefore, are what they are because they received their forms through a divine mythical act.[11] The story of creation, of course, is found in the Tetrateuch, but it is not archetypal, at least not for Israel as Israel. The archetypal period of Israel was the forty years, the time when she was created as the people of the Lord within history already existing.

In the Tetrateuch, therefore, the order of myth and history is reversed. Myth is not primary; it does not stand at the beginning of all things, it is not the foundation of natural life, but a certain part of history is transposed into the mythical. If it is accepted that any story in which a divine actor has a part is a myth, then it also must be accepted that whatever historical events stand behind the now-exaggerated stories of the exodus and the Sinai event, those events were made mythological; that is, they were interpreted as events in which God was an actor and in which he had entered history. A good example is Moses. His historical person disappeared almost totally behind the mythological motifs. He may have been a man of great intellectual capacity, a talented leader, and a religious genius. But if he was, we know nothing about him as such. In the Tetrateuch he is merely a mediator of God, a man through whom God acted. As far as his function is concerned, he is a mythological figure.

This method of transposing real history to the plane of the mythological is detectable everywhere in the Bible. David's life, whatever it may have been, became an opportunity to declare that in his time God did something important for his people. David also became a mythological figure in an Israelite manner, through whom God secured the life of Israel as Israel. In the figure and life story of Jesus of Nazareth, the same tendency can be observed. The New Testament admits that he was not, that is, not for every individual, a man through whom God was at work; that he was not the Messiah, Son of God, Son of Man, except for those who could recognize him as such. In other words, he was looked upon as God's servant for man's salvation only by those who could see him as a mythological figure in history. Of course, speaking in this way, calling the biblical story a myth, one runs the risk of grave misunderstanding. But, once again, if we consider that all events can be called mythological which speak about divine acts and interventions —and in the Bible we read about divine interventions in history—then there will be no reason for offense. If this is understood, then the statement that the biblical story is mythological will appear as a statement spoken in the language of comparative religion, yet having the same meaning as the Christian truth spoken in the language of faith; it will mean that God intervened for the sake of man in history.

The other difference between the archetypal period of Israel and that of other religions, especially those in the primitive stage, is that it was not a time when culture and civilization were established. The Lord is not a high god of primitive religion who at the beginning of things taught man the elements of culture. Neither is Moses a culture hero. Nothing is said about humanity having lived under barbarous conditions, about the teaching of the art of farming, building houses, and the like. The Tetrateuch assumes that during the exodus and the wilderness wanderings culture and civilization were already in existence and, therefore, during her archetypal period Israel was not created into a nation of culture but a nation of holiness. At that time she received a particular quality, a new power of life from the Lord which made her distinct from all other nations.[12]

Of course, the nature of this qualified life, this holiness, is conceived in just about the same manner as the impersonal force in other religions. In this respect the Tetrateuch reflects the same ideas as the surrounding nations. Holiness is, therefore, contagious and so is impurity (Lev. 6:18, 27; 11:32; 16:23, 26, etc.), yet to be in possession of the first and to avoid the second is important because otherwise communion with the Lord is impossible. Similar concepts are also found in the New Testament, and through them, both Testaments express the same thing—the sacramental nature of biblical religion. This idea, the idea that Israel received and now possesses a particular quality from the Lord, is found especially in a certain collection of laws called by scholars the Code of Holiness (Lev. 17-26), but it is also found elsewhere (Lev. 11:44 ff.).

> You shall be holy to me; for I the LORD am holy, and have separated you from the peoples, that you should be mine (Lev. 20:26).

The sacrifices and the purificatory rites, ordered in the archetypal time, serve, therefore, as a restoration of holiness and thereby restoration to communion with the Lord. What is said of Israel in Leviticus 4:13, 20b, is valid for both private individuals and the public personage of a ruler.

> If the whole congregation of Israel commits a sin unwittingly . . . and they do any one of the things which the LORD has commanded not to be done and are guilty . . .

then a sacrifice has to be brought to the Lord and the result will be "the priest shall make atonement for them, and they shall be forgiven" (cf. Lev. 4:2, 22; 6:2, 7; 12:7; 14:19, 25, 29; Num. 5:5-8). Thus not life in its natural form, as pure physical existence, is the purpose of the cultic rites—not health, fertility, wealth, or success—but the purpose is qualified holy life, making one fit for togetherness with the Lord.

The physical gifts are, of course, from him too. However, they do not depend on the performance of certain rites, but on obedience, on the willingness to live according to the divine design; for life, the law, and the gifts are withdrawn if the design is not followed.

> If you walk in my statutes and observe my commandments and do them, then I will give you your rains in their season, and the land shall yield its increase . . . But if you will not hearken to me, and will not do all these commandments . . . I will break the pride of your power, and I will make your heavens like iron and your earth like brass . . . for your land shall not yield its increase (Lev. 26:3-4, 14, 19-20).

The nature of the archetypal law of Israel is also different from the ethical order of other religions. In the Tetrateuch we search vainly for the idea of a "basic value" (*Grundwert*), a force which permeates all humanity and the entire cosmos, as the Egyptian Maat, or whatever names the inherent force giving order and meaning to the cosmos was called among other nations. Of course, a similar idea is found in the canonical and non-canonical wisdom literature of Israel and Judaism, but not in the Tetrateuch. In the wisdom literature, *chokma*, wisdom, was created in the beginning; God created the world through it and it permeates the all (Prov. 3:19; 8:19 ff.; Job 12:13; 28:23 ff.; Ecclus. 1; 24:3 ff., etc.). It is personified; as a matter of fact, the personification is so strong that it may be considered almost as the intrusion of polytheism (Prov. 1:20 ff.; 8:2 ff.; 9:1 ff.; Ecclus. 14:20 ff.; 24:1; Wisd. of Sol. 9:10). It can be shared by kings and wise men of all nations (Prov. 8:15 ff.; 28:2), and it gives knowledge, true life, and good luck to all (Prov. 4:9; 8:18; Eccl. 10:10; Ecclus. 1:18, etc.).

But, as is well known, even though this idea of wisdom as the ground of right conduct may have been known to Israel in ancient times, its knowledge was restricted to a few, the members of the higher, learned class. True, after the captivity it became prominent for a short time and even had some formal influence on Old Testament literature, but eventually it was rejected by both Judaism and Christianity. It may also be admitted that the authors of the Old Testament books were some sort of wise men—after all, they were educated, and the wise men constituted the educated class of the ancient Near East—but most of them were not identical with those wise men who believed in an archetypal force inherent in the cosmos. The idea of inherent wisdom is absent in the Tetrateuch; its author was not one of those who believed in it. According to him, wisdom, as the inner ability of man, was restricted to the craftsmen (Exod. 28:3; 31:2 ff.).

The idea of holiness mentioned above is by no means identical with wisdom created in the archetypal time as an inherent principle of cosmic and social order. It is not the possession of all mankind; it is a specific quality of Israel. Good conduct, therefore, is not the natural outflow of wisdom as a force inherent in man, but is prescribed by the statutory law. Throughout the legal collections in the Book of the Covenant and the Code of Holiness (Exod. 20-23; Lev. 17-26), it is assumed that man has no "wisdom"; therefore, he is not able to determine what the good acts are, but he has to be told what the good is. In this context one might say that according to Israelite law, wisdom is the will of God, who had given the commandments of good conduct. There is, therefore, no archetypal "basic value" in the Tetrateuch, but there are archetypal commandments which have to be kept forever.

In the present Tetrateuch there is no trace of the repetition of mythical events for the purpose of releasing the primeval energy. At this point, of course, the feasts of Israel should be mentioned, at which, if there was anything like that in the mind of the author, these semi-magical repetitions should have occurred. Yet in studying the cultic calendar as found in Leviticus 23 and Numbers 28:16—29:40, we find nothing like that. Three convictions appear in these passages and all of them are typically Israelite. The first is that the source of all blessings of the field is the Lord and not the baals. True, we find rites which suggest the presence of primitive ideas. One is the offering of the sheaf, another is the offering of the two loaves of bread (Lev. 23:9 ff., 15 ff.). A third rite, or rather practice, was that at harvest the grain on the edge of the field had to be left standing and no gleaning was permitted. In its Canaanite context—for it is certain that the practice was adopted from the Canaanites—this was done either to placate the fertility numen or on the principle that nothing should be fully exhausted in order that what is left may increase again. In the present context, however, the rites of the sheaf and of the two loaves bring about the desacralization of the new crop, and part of the grain has to be left on the field for the poor and the stranger (Lev. 23:22; cf. Deut. 24:19). None of these three rites release the sacred, impersonal energy.

The second specific Israelite idea appearing in the cultic calendar is that the feasts are commemorations of saving acts, particularly those of the exodus. Thus, the Passover and the Feast of Booths are to be kept to remember the deliverance from Egypt (Exod. 12:17; Lev. 23:43). Perhaps, at this point there was a feeling analogous to releasing the sacred energy by reenacting myths. After all, both the rites of the Passover and the practice of living in booths were repetitions. Yet there is no trace that either one meant the release of primeval energy. Being reminders of God's saving acts, both simply strengthened the hope that the Lord would do in the future what he had done in the past.

The third conviction in the cultic calendar finds its expression in the rites of the day of atonement, celebrated at the end of the New Year festival. At first sight the rites suggest renewal, but a closer inspection reveals that they effect purification, removing the uncleanness which would mean exclusion from the communion with the Lord. Thus even the New Year festival did not mean the release of primeval energy in Israel. Even if it is admitted that, after the pattern of the Babylonian *akitu* festival, perhaps in the form of the enthronement of the Lord or of the royal Zion festival, there were elements in the New Year feast which were mythical repetitions and resulted in the release of that energy,[13] these elements are totally lacking from the present descriptions. Perhaps before the captivity, the idea that the energy could be released by ritual acts was known. But this idea was suppressed by the author, and the fact that he suppressed it is important. Why did he suppress it? He did it because he could not accept the belief that by repetition of mythical acts the impersonal energy was renewed either in nature or in history.

Finally, the cultic rites, commanded by the Tetrateuch, are not mythical repetitions and therefore do not derive their effectiveness in this way. None of them have the same meaning as the rite of India enacting the reconquest of the cosmos by Soma in the primeval time. Of course, these rites are archetypes to be repeated and are statutes to be followed forever. Yet they are efficacious not by mere repetition but because the Lord had ordered them. In their Canaanite form, they may have been of such nature; but in the present context, if one really seeks parallels, they are similar to isolated magic rites, with the difference that their efficacy is not because of the impersonal power but because the Lord gives them efficacy.

What is the reason for these differences? Undoubtedly, the reason that the myth is not the source of history but history is transposed into the mythical is that Israel's religion is a religion of revelation. There are parallels to this idea in other religions that also consider themselves as religions of revelation. For all such religions, part of history became myth because the period when the receiver of revelation lived was a time qualified by the specific presence of the divine. There are not many religions of this type, and one can name them easily. All believe that at a certain point of datable history God, by revealing himself to a concrete individual, intervened and communicated the "truth" for man's salvation. Such religions are—besides Old Testament religion and Judaism—Zoroastrianism, Christianity, Islam, and, in a sense, Buddhism.[14] The difference between them and Israel's religion is that according to the latter the revelation was given to one nation alone and is now available to all who by decision accept the revealed truth.

In the particular situation of the Old Testament writers, this is understandable. The present Old Testament books were produced in order to give a program for restored Israel and to encourage her among the nations who threatened her with absorption and her religion with dissolution in syncretism. Israel, therefore, had to be distinguished sharply from all other nations. Revelation came to her and to no one else. This also explains why the author of the Tetrateuch insisted on a specific holiness, a peculiar quality given to Israel alone in her archetypal period which had nothing to do with the power inherent in nature. This particular holiness distinguished Israel from all other nations and give the guarantee that she was set apart from the rest of humanity.

The rest of the differences between the archetypal thinking of Israel and of other nations—that there is no "basic value," an inherent force in nature and society which creates order in the cosmos and which regulates human conduct; that there are no reenactments of myths for the purpose of releasing primeval energy; and that the cultic rites are not efficacious by mere repetition—find their explanation in the unique nature of Israel's God. He is not a force inherent in nature and society but a God acting continuously in history. Strictly speaking, he is not a person in the Greek sense but a function, acting all the time for the good of his people. He controls all things. The physical order is maintained and the moral order is set by his statutory law forever. There is no room, therefore, for an ability in man by which he would be capable of perfect moral conduct. The nature of this God excludes also the idea of releasing primeval energy by reenacting myths, because what that energy would do is already being done by him. Finally, the archetypal cultic rites are not efficacious in themselves or because they are repetitions of mythical acts. The Lord's will is to keep Israel within the divine realm or to restore it to his fellowship; therefore, he commanded these rites and his sovereign power gives them efficacy.

Thus, then, with these differences, the author made the ancient, perhaps primitive pattern of the archetype his basic didactic method, and thereby he gave weight to everything he proclaimed. His audience lived in a world where reference to archetypes and teaching through them was commonplace. Everyone who read his work, or heard it interpreted in Israel, agreed with him: If it is true that God appeared "once upon a time," in the time of the patriarchs or Moses, to create us into a nation, then we stand indeed on a sure foundation; if at that time we received a qualified life, holiness, then we are privileged among all nations. And if the law was given in the archetypal period and teaches us a form of life which is pleasing to God, that law should never be changed but obeyed always. And if the cult, established "once upon a time," is efficacious by God's will and restores us to his fellowship, it must be performed. The entire Mosaic tradition, a result of slow growth, a result of a forward movement in history, obtained divine authority by being represented as archetypal.

All this may be admitted about the positive archetypal

elements, that is, about those elements of Mosaic tradition which expressed beliefs and asked for institutions which the author wanted to establish in restored Israel. These elements were (to repeat what has already been said) those stories, legal and cultic precepts, which proclaimed the beliefs that God had intervened in history in the archetypal period, and thereby created Israel, that this nation received a qualified life, that it was protected and provided for by the Lord, that there was a divine law, and that the cult was divinely established. But why did the author tell the rebellion stories? After all, they did not speak about archetypal truths to be accepted, about examples to be followed; they did not illustrate laws to be followed, but they spoke about examples to be shunned. These stories expressed condemnation of the fathers, the ancestors who, as a rule, were revered by all nations. Why was Israel, who spoke through the mouth of the author, an exception?

We have seen the historical reasons why these stories were remembered and further developed, and we also attempted to analyze the motif in its various forms in Old Testament literature. The historical reason was the condemnation of the nation's idolatrous past, and we have seen that the motif served as a didactic method for various authors. Now, in the light of what has been said about the archetypal nature of Mosaic tradition, it can be stated that in these stories the Tetrateuchal author did the same thing that the rest of the Old Testament writers did: He presented the fathers, the rebellious generation, as a *negative archetype,* one *not* to be followed, and by other elements of the motif he encouraged his generation, the generation of the restoration, with the ready help of the Lord and proclaimed his unconditional grace.

What has already been touched upon in the introduction may be repeated. With the stories of the golden calf and of

Baal-Peor, he warned against idolatry, which at his time still was a real threat for Judaism. With the "murmuring" stories, on the one hand, he proclaimed that those who were reluctant to accept the hardships that went with the work of the restoration would be punished by the Lord, and on the other, he encouraged them to expect his help. Finally, with the story of the spies, declaring the divine verdict that the wilderness generation could not enter the land of promise and expressing the belief that the Lord's saving will cannot be resisted, he proclaimed that if his own generation were unwilling to go along with the divine plan, their sons would reach the goal.

Indeed, the Tetrateuch does not present history "as it actually happened," and the rebellion stories are not told for the sake of historical information. It is a work with a purpose. That purpose was to present the Mosaic tradition as archetypal, having eternal validity, and in the author's hand the rebellion stories served as means to strengthen that validity. He knew, or he took it for granted, that whatever happened in the archetypal period was tremendously important for all succeeding generations. Life must be shaped according to what happened then; what was accepted at that time must be accepted now, and what was rejected must be rejected forever. The picture he drew of the archetypal age would, indeed, be much less impressive and his message weakened without the rebellion stories.

Finally, a few words about the function of the Mosaic tradition in the preservation of Israel centuries before the appearance of Christianity, a function which has been seen by many scholars but, perhaps, not in its full significance. This tradition served as a reintegrating force for Judaism in the midst of an incipient syncretism. Most scholars speak about cultural and religious syncretism only after the emergence of Hellenism. True, syncretism reached its peak after Alexander the Great, but its roots go back as far as the beginnings of the Persian empire. The Mosaic tradition, as it appears in the Tetrateuch, counteracted the forces of incipient syncretism, and when Hellenism emerged, it found restored Israel, i.e., Judaism, already as a group with uniform convictions. Even if the statement is somewhat forced, it may be said that Judaism entered its Middle Ages—that is, an age of uniformity and social compactness and strength—with the publication of the Tetrateuch, the written form of Mosaic tradition. At the time of the Hellenistic and Roman empires this was a unique phenomenon, not found in any other nation or cult. Hellenism and Hellenistic Judaism in its Christian form reached this stage too, but not until more than a millennium later.

If it is true that Israelite law helped Old Israel to preserve its identity before the exile,[15] it is even more true that without the Mosaic tradition Judaism would have disappeared completely. The so-called intertestamental period, between the restoration and the birth of Jesus, therefore, was not a truly creative age, at least not for normative Judaism. The truly creative age was the age during which the Tetrateuch was produced in its present form, and the intertestamental period was a time during which the Torah tradition gradually permeated all tissues of Jewish life. Of course, the intertestamental period was also creative to some extent. It produced Jewish groups showing signs of syncretism—Hellenistic Judaism, apocalyptic sects, and possibly gnostic groups—but these groups were on the periphery. Not these groups but the author of the Tetrateuch represented the truly creative spirit. He was responsible for the reintegration of Judaism and for the emergence of its normative form which proved indestructible. He laid the foundations, and the foundations were lasting.

5
THE REBELLION MOTIF
OUTSIDE THE TETRATEUCH

The above discussion of the use of the rebellion stories by the editor of the Tetrateuch and his didactic purpose would be nothing but a shaky theory were these considerations not supported by the presence and use of the same motif in biblical passages outside the Tetrateuch. But references to the sins and rebellions of the fathers are found in a great number of other books, with the difference that not only the rebellions during the exodus are mentioned but also the sins of the post-conquest fathers. This is natural. Since the Old Testament books, as they now stand before us, came from the hand of the post-exilic generation, and since the conviction established firmly by the preaching of the pre-exilic prophets that the Lord was the strongest of the gods, perhaps the only one, could not be given up, the Old Testament books in their present form explain the tragedy of the exile by saying: It was not the Lord's defeat by the gods of Babylon, but a punishment imposed by him for the sins of the fathers, of the times both before and after the conquest.

This element in the motif, reference to the sins of the post-conquest fathers, appears even in the early prophets, writing soon after the age of the Omrides (876-842 B.C.). Amos, the first of the prophets whose utterances were preserved, charging his people with idolatry, says, "their lies have led them astray, after which their fathers walked" (2:4b). Hosea, writing soon after the Omrides to the idolatrous post-conquest fathers of the North, refers only to the sins of the wilderness generation; but Isaiah, calling the people of his own time "offspring of evildoers," probably refers to the bad example of the post-conquest fathers (1:4). Shortly before the exile, Jeremiah mentions them several times. The Lord asks,

> What wrong did your fathers find in me
>   that they went far from me,
> and went after worthlessness, and became worthless?
> They did not say, "Where is the LORD
>   who brought us up from the land of Egypt . . ." (2:5-6a).

In referring to the burning of incense in the streets of Jerusalem, he could not have in mind the fathers of the wilderness wanderings (44:21; cf. 7:25; 9:14; 11:7).

The idea that the exile was a punishment for the sins of the pre-captivity generation becomes, then, commonplace in the later Old Testament books. A classic example is found in Zechariah 1:4-6:

> Be not like your fathers, to whom the former prophets cried out, "Thus says the LORD of hosts, Return from your evil ways and from your evil deeds." But they did not hear or heed me, says the LORD. Your fathers, where are they? And the prophets, do they live for ever? But my words and statutes, which I commanded my servants the prophets, did they not overtake your fathers? (Cf. Isa. 43:27 f.; Jer. 3:24 ff.; 2 Chron. 36:15; Ezra 5:12; Neh. 13:18; Dan. 9:11).

Eventually the post-conquest fathers are joined with the fathers of the wilderness and become also negative archetypes. In the work of the Chronicler the warning put into the mouth of Hezekiah addressing the remnants of the northern tribes illustrates this.

> Do not be like your fathers and your brethren, who were faithless to the LORD God of their fathers, so that he made them a desolation, as you see (2 Chron. 30:7).

However, whether or not the two generations are joined together, whenever the motif appears outside the Tetrateuch, there is always one difference. Whereas the Tetrateuch, actually written to teach the post-exilic generation yet intending to give the impression that the author was telling the "authentic" story of the wilderness wanderings, could only imply the didactic purpose, elsewhere that purpose is clear. We find four forms. First, the *negative archetype* with two sub-forms: one, the *pure negative archetype,* implying the warning, "do not do as the fathers did"; the other, the *direct charge* that those who are addressed are following the bad example of the fathers. Second, the *confession of sins,* stating directly or indirectly that those who are now acknowledging their sins will not imitate the fathers. Third, the *rebellious history,* representing Israel's history as a series of rebellions, which implies that from now on history will be free of rebellions. Fourth, a form which may be called the *in-spite-of* form, acknowledging the fathers' sins, yet proclaiming that they were always forgiven and expressing the hope that it will be so in the future.

The Book of the Conquest is typical for the first form, the *negative archetype.* Its first part, which is now Deuteronomy, is presented as a long sermon delivered by Moses, supposedly to teach the generation about ready to enter Canaan. As we have seen, actually the work was addressed to Israel shortly after or during the Canaanite resurgence, and its intention was to give a program for restoration in the ninth century. The proposed historical situation and the actual intention of the author explain why the motif is used openly in a didactic way. In the original introduction to the Book of the Conquest, where just about all the rebellion stories found in the Tetrateuch are mentioned (Deut. 4-11), the motif is used in this way several times. In 6:16 the author says: "You shall not put the LORD your God to the test, as you tested him at Massah." In 8:11 ff. the same warning, do not do as the fathers did, is in mind. It refers to the "fiery serpents," the "flinty rock," the "manna" (Exod. 16; 17; Num. 21) and reminds its audience that Israel was rebuked on those occasions by the Lord, "that he might humble you and test you" (vs. 16). The long story of the golden calf, told with many variations from the Tetrateuch (Deut. 6:6—10:21), is recited in order that the author may utter the warning: "Circumcise therefore the foreskin of your heart, and be no longer stubborn" (10:16). The tradition about the sin of Dathan and Abiram, mentioned without Korah the Levite, is referred to in 11:6, with no information as to what their sin was. It is, no doubt, a negative archetype, because it underlines the warning to keep the Lord's "charge, his statutes, his ordinances, and his commandments" (vs. 1), and threatens the violators with the same punishment.[1] The rest of the Deuteronomic History also knows about the rebellious history (to be analyzed later). Only Joshua 22:17 mentions as negative archetype the sin with Baal-Peor. The passage is in a late haggadic story about the building of an altar east of the Jordan by the Reubenites, Gadites, and the half tribe of Manasseh.

The early prophets, Amos and Hosea, also know about the rebellious fathers, but again in the form of the rebellious history, while Psalms 78 and 106 mention it in the in-spite-of form. But some Psalms assuming the form of prophetic warning are familiar with the motif as a negative archetype. Although it is not clear, in Psalm 81:7 the reference is probably of this nature. In Psalm 99:8, where mention is made that the Lord was the avenger of Moses' and Aaron's wrongdoings, the incident is a negative archetype because the two leaders are referred to as examples of divine punishment. The best known Psalm passage where the motif appears as a negative archetype is 95:7b-9:

> O that today you would hearken to his voice!
>   Harden not your hearts, as at Meribah
>   as on the day at Massah in the wilderness,
> when your fathers tested me,
>   and put me to the proof, though they had seen my work.

The negative archetype of the fathers emerges again in the post-exilic literature, in Zechariah 1:4 ff. and in 2 Chronicles

30:7. In both instances not only the wilderness fathers but also the post-conquest fathers become examples not to be followed. Finally, the late post-exilic passage in Jeremiah 17: 22 ff. also mentions the fathers in the "do not do as they did" form.

The same negative archetype is used frequently in a sub-form, within or without the prophetic collections. The sub-form is a *charge* made by some authors that their contemporaries are imitating the fathers. A classic example is part of the Deuter-onomistic sermon in 2 Kings 17:14-15a, telling that, although the prophets warned them, the Northern Kingdom fell because they followed the fathers:

> . . . they would not listen, but were stubborn, as their fathers had been, who did not believe in the LORD their God.

This form was known as early as Hosea, who charged that the fathers had already turned to Baal-Peor at the time when Israel was found by the Lord as "the first fruit on the fig tree, in its first season" (9:10); then, assuming tacitly that the descendants are doing the same, he goes on and threatens Ephraim with destruction.

The form is much favored by Jeremiah. In 7:21-26 we read that although the command was given to the fathers "Obey my voice, and I will be your God, and you shall be my people . . . they did not obey or incline their ear, but walked in their own counsels . . . and went backward and not forward." Then, meaning his own generation, he declares, "They did worse than their fathers." Again, in 9:13 ff., written probably at the time when the countryside was already conquered by Nebu-chadnezzar and only Jerusalem was standing, the prophet predicts the dispersion because the people "have gone after the Baals, as their fathers taught them." In 11:9-12 he once again predicts Judah's destruction because, "They have turned back to the iniquities of their forefathers." In 16:11-12, in explain-ing why the calamities came upon the people, he quotes the

Lord: "Because your fathers have forsaken me . . . and have gone after other gods . . . and because you have done worse than your fathers . . ." The imitation of the sinful deeds of the fathers is implied in 34:13-22. There, in referring not to the present Tetrateuch but to the Sinai tradition known to him somewhat differently, Jeremiah reminds his people of the obligation of setting free the Hebrew slaves in the seventh year (Exod. 21:2), which neither they nor their fathers have kept. Ezekiel also knows the form. In 20:30 he charges the "house of Israel": "Will you defile yourselves after the manner of your fathers [probably post-conquest fathers are meant] and go astray after their detestable things?"

In summary: The negative archetype of the rebellious fathers, both in the form of a warning, "do not do as the fathers did," and in the form of a charge that the generation addressed imitate them, serves the purpose of attempting to ensure that similar sins will not be committed any more. They underline the positive archetypes, the commands given in the Tetrateuch and known to the writers in some form, and call for loyalty to the Lord.

The rebellious fathers are frequently mentioned in *confessions of sins*. They all show a feeling of corporate responsibility in the spirit of the well-known third commandment, "I the LORD your God am a jealous God, visiting the iniquity of the fathers upon the children." Deuteronomy, in addressing the second generation, ready to enter Canaan, takes it for granted that they were present at Sinai, and that, as members of the same corporate personality, they are identical with the first generation (Deut. 1:9, 26; 4:3; 6:16, etc.). In post-exilic confessions this feeling of identity is especially strong when it is admitted that the reason for the captivity was the sin of the fathers. One example in the prayer of Ezra will speak for all:

> O my God, I am ashamed and blush to lift my face to thee, my God, for our iniquities have risen higher than our heads, and our

guilt has mounted up to the heavens. From the days of our fathers to this day we have been in great guilt; and for our iniquities we, our kings, and our priests have been given into the hand of the kings of the lands, to the sword, to captivity, to plundering, and to utter shame, as at this day (Ezra 9:6-7).

A very similar confession is found as part of a prayer, ascribed also to Ezra by the Greek translation, in Nehemiah 9:32-37 (cf. Ezra 5:12; Neh. 1:5 ff.; Ps. 79:8; Jer. 3:24-25).

The strongest and bitterest form of the motif is the form of the *rebellious history*. It regards Israel's history—beginning with the fathers of Egypt, through the post-conquest generation, up until the time of the authors—as a series of rebellions. The Book of the Conquest already knows this form. Deuteronomy 9:7 says, "from the day you came out of the land of Egypt, until you came to this place, you have been rebellious against the LORD." In a later addition the motif appears as a forewarning of coming sins:

> . . . I know how rebellious and stubborn you are; behold, while I [i.e., Moses] am yet alive with you, today you have been rebellious against the LORD; how much more after my death! (Deut. 31:27).

This form began to emerge soon after Omri and Jehu, in Hosea. The famous second chapter, which for the first time conceives the relationship of the Lord and Israel as husband and wife, is already familiar with the theme that Israel sinned from the beginning. It speaks about Israel's birth in the "parched land," i.e., the wilderness, and goes on telling of her idolatries. Chapter 9 speaks about the sin with Baal-Peor and implies that the present worship of Baal is the continuation of the same sin (vs. 10). In 11:1-2, then, the charge is sounded clearly:

> When Israel was a child, I loved him,
>   and out of Egypt I called my son.
> The more I called them,
>   the more they went from me;
> they kept sacrificing to the Baals,
>   and burning incense to idols.

Essentially the same is told in 13:4 ff., where the prophet complains that although the Lord was Israel's God from the land of Egypt, when "they were filled . . . they forgot me" (vs. 6).

Second Isaiah too, who hardly ever mentions the rebellion motif, knows about Israel that "from birth you were called a rebel" (48:8b). Jeremiah raises the same charge in his long prophetic sermon in 2:4-37, spoken mainly against alliance with the great powers (vs. 18). Israel's fathers, he says, found wrong in the Lord. When they were brought into a plentiful land, in turning to alien gods, they "made my heritage an abomination," thus doing something no nation ever did (vss. 4, 7, 11). He continues his rebuke in 7:25-26:

> From the day that your fathers came out of the land of Egypt to this day, I have persistently sent all my servants the prophets to them, day after day; yet they did not listen to me, or incline their ear, but stiffened their neck. They did worse than their fathers.

The same is repeated in 11:7 f., reminding the people that although the fathers were solemnly and persistently warned since Egypt "even to this day," "they did not obey . . . but every one walked in the stubbornness of his evil heart."

The Deuteronomic History also views Israel's history as a series of rebellions. The theme appears first in the answer of the Lord to Samuel concerning the people's request for a king. The Lord says that the request is one of the rebellions committed "from the day I brought them up out of Egypt" (1 Sam. 8:8). Written by a Judean hand, this reason is, of course, quoted for the fall of the Northern Kingdom in 2 Kings 17:7 ff. But because of her rebellions Judah must also fall:

> And I will cast off the remnant of my heritage, and give them into the hand of their enemies . . . because they have done what is evil in my sight and have provoked me to anger, since the day their fathers came out of Egypt, even to this day (2 Kings 21: 14-15).

As the Deuteronomic author believes, even Josiah, the pious king, was compelled to acknowledge that

> great is the wrath of the LORD that is kindled against us, because our fathers have not obeyed the words of this book, to do according to all that is written concerning us (2 Kings 22:13).

The book of Ezekiel has the same view of Israel's history. The charge is made first in 2:3:

> Son of man, I send you to the people of Israel, to a nation of rebels, who have rebelled against me; they and their fathers have transgressed against me to this very day.

He fully develops the theme in three long passages, 16:8-63, 20:3-44, and in chapter 23. But since in the first two passages not only the sinful history of Israel is rebuked but also the in-spite-of form appears, we shall deal with them later.

In chapter 23, however, the prophet makes no mention of the divine grace. With vivid imagination he tells the sinful history of the two kingdoms of Israel personified as two sisters and two wives of the Lord, Oholah and Oholibah (vss. 4 ff.). Where this analogy, rather strange for the religion of Israel, originated is difficult to tell. Perhaps it was borrowed from the Canaanite religion in which the fertility goddesses were the wives of Baal, and was changed to fit the Israelite religion. Ezekiel may have adopted it from Hosea who, as has been mentioned, was the first to use the analogy of husband and wife to characterize the relationship of the Lord and Israel, or he may have developed it independently.

At any rate, with a language hardly acceptable to our more refined taste but with great poetic power, he describes first the "adultery," i.e., idolatry, of Oholah (i.e., Samaria) in Egypt. Then he tells about the "adulteries" of Samaria with the Assyrian gods and states that "judgment had been executed upon her" (23:5-10). In turning to Oholibah (i.e., Jerusalem) he also refers to her playing the harlot in Egypt and then tells about her "adulteries" with the Assyrians and Babylonians.

Finally, he pronounces judgment upon Jerusalem in saying that precisely those "lovers" will destroy her (vs. 22). Indeed, the entire chapter is witness that the prophet saw nothing good either in Samaria or in Jerusalem; their history appeared to him as a defiant rebellion against the Lord. The passage ends with the declaration of irrevocable judgment upon Judah:

> Bring up a host against them, and make them an object of terror and a spoil. . . . And your lewdness shall be requited upon you, and you shall bear the penalty for your sinful idolatry; and you shall know that I am the Lord GOD (Ezek. 23:46, 49).

The story of Oholah and Oholibah was written before the fall of Jerusalem—that is, before the beginning of the exile. Two other passages, however, written after the return, show that it was customary for the generation of the restoration to view the pre-exilic history of Israel as a continuous rebellion. One passage is in the already-mentioned Zechariah 1:4, where the post-captivity fathers are mentioned as bad examples. The other is in Malachi 3:7, where the stereotyped saying occurs: "From the days of your fathers you have turned aside from my statutes and have not kept them."

The most important form of the negative archetypes, the rebellious fathers, is the *in-spite-of* form, which proclaims that though the fathers have sinned—and so has the present generation—God has forgiven both. As we have seen, the proclamation of the divine grace was important also for the stories of the Tetrateuch.

In a conditional form, that is, on the condition that the people return to the Lord forgiveness and blessing will follow, this archetype appears in the Deuteronomic History. As a matter of fact, as a didactic element, this is the central message of the great work. The long sermon in Judges 2:11 ff., actually preaching to the generation in the captivity, mentions the example of the post-conquest fathers, tells how they "forsook the LORD," "went after other gods," how they were punished by invading enemies, how they cried to the Lord, and then, as a result, how they were delivered by the hand of the judges. The theme is the same in another sermon in 1 Samuel 12:6 ff. First it mentions the deliverance from Egypt, then speaking of the post-conquest fathers, tells that because they forgot the Lord, they were punished by the hand of Sisera, the Philistines, and Moab. As the sermon in Judges 2, it also states that when they cried to the Lord, they were helped.

Following in the footsteps of the Deuteronomist, the Chronicler proclaims the same truth. In his prayer, Nehemiah first confesses that "I and my father's house have sinned. We have acted very corruptly against thee" (1:6, 7). Then, in reference to Deuteronomy 4:27, 30 ff., he mentions the need for return, that Israel may be gathered from the dispersion. Some Psalm passages also know this form. Psalm 81:7 refers to Meribah and admonishes the people to listen to the Lord. Psalm 99:6 ff. recalls Moses, Aaron, and Samuel, who had called upon the Lord's name and, although he was an "avenger of their wrongdoings," he had answered them. The lesson is clear: If the present generation follows the example of the sinful yet repenting fathers, the Lord's forgiveness is certain.

The unconditional grace of God in spite of rebellions is then proclaimed in a few but important passages indicating that for didactic purposes this form was believed the most effective. There are six passages to be considered: Deuteronomy 9:4—10:22; Ezekiel 16; 20; Psalms 78; 106; and Nehemiah 9:4-37.

In Deuteronomy 9:4—10:22 the motif takes up the greater part of one of the many sermons in the book. Its main theme is:

> Know therefore, that the LORD your God is not giving you this good land to possess because of your righteousness; for you are a stubborn people. Remember and do not forget how you provoked

the LORD your God to wrath in the wilderness; from the day you came out of the land of Egypt, until you came to this place, you have been rebellious against the Lord (9:6-7).

Then it goes on telling the rebellion stories, first the rebellion with the golden calf, at length, and mentioning Taberah, Massah (i.e., Meribah), and Kibroth-hattaavah (9:22). Twice it refers to the intercession of Moses to which the gracious answer of the Lord was to issue the ten commandments the second time. The divine forgiveness is proclaimed thus:

. . . the LORD was unwilling to destroy you. And the LORD said to me, "Arise, go on your journey at the head of the people, that they may go in and possess the land, which I swore to their fathers to give them" (10:10b-11).

Finally, it is declared that in spite of the rebellions, "the LORD set his heart in love upon your fathers and chose their descendants after them, you above all peoples" (10:15). In brief: The moral is brought home. There was sin and rebellion, but this did not change God's plan and love. The people are here; the Lord had kept his promise:

Your fathers went down to Egypt seventy persons; and now the LORD your God has made you as the stars of heaven for multitude (10:22).

The duty of the people is now to obey:

You shall fear the LORD your God; you shall serve him and cleave to him, and by his name you shall swear (10:20).

The next two passages are found in Ezekiel. The first, chapter 16, describes, just as does chapter 23, Israel's history as a series of rebellions. Since it does not mention the sin of the wilderness fathers one may, perhaps, object to its being considered in this context. It knows nothing about the patriarchal traditions either, and it seems to view Israel's early history as an age of perfect loyalty. Yet, because its essence is a warning against imitating the sins of the pre-captivity fathers and because at the end it proclaims God's grace unconditionally, it has a place here.

There are some other peculiarities also. It implies that Israel was not born in Egypt or at Sinai but in Canaan, that her father was an Amorite and her mother a Hittite, i.e., Israel was born from the union of two groups of these nations (Ezek. 16:3, 45b). Another peculiar statement says that Samaria not only was the sister of Jerusalem but also of Sodom, the city famed for its sins, and ascribes to the latter not only the sin of sodomy but also ruthlessness and pride (vs. 49). Apparently, this tradition held that Sodom was not destroyed as described in Genesis 19 but by enemies (vs. 53).

The unity of the passage is also questionable. It is believed that for the basis of his sermon the prophet used a folktale or a wisdom haggada illustrating the miserable fate of adulterous wives. Supposedly the story began by telling about an unwanted female infant set out by her mother (vs. 5)—apparently a harlot herself (vs. 43b)—a custom generally practiced in ancient times. This child was found by a god or magician and kept alive by his magic word (vs. 6). She was met again later by the healer, who married her and lifted her to royal standing. The tale then told about her shameful adulteries and eventual cruel punishment (vss. 38 ff.). It is also believed that originally only the judgment was proclaimed and that vss. 59 ff., about the "everlasting covenant," are later additions. Whatever the case may be, the details are interesting only secondarily for the interpretation.

However, it may be noted that the tradition about Sodom, not known elsewhere, is not necessarily from a second hand, and the "tale" may also be the original creation of the prophet.[2] The passage about the "everlasting covenant" may, indeed, be secondary, but since biblical interpretation, unless important reasons prevent it, deals with the text as it stands now, this detail may be left aside. Otherwise the chapter is of some archeological interest. It gives information about how ancient harlots, considered as representatives of the fertility goddess, practiced their trade by setting up their "vaulted chambers" at the head of every street and square (vs. 31) and accepting hire, and about how adulterous wives were punished, first by displaying them naked to the public and then by cutting them in pieces to give a terrifying example (vss. 39-40).[3]

What is interesting for us here is the message the prophet proclaims. As he sees it, from the time when she became the people of the Lord, Israel's history was nothing but continuous disloyalty. Everything she had, she received from her husband, the Lord. She received from him her high standing among the nations, her wealth, her plenitude of food, her sons and daughters—i.e., that she was a nation of many people (vss. 14-20). Yet she turned to other gods—first to the gods of the Canaanites in practicing their child sacrifice, then to the gods of the Egyptians, Assyrians, and Chaldeans (vss. 20-28). She topped all this with two unbelievable sins. First, she never remembered her low status before she became the Lord's people, i.e., she never scrutinized her past (vs. 22); second, although she received everything from the Lord, she gave all his gifts to gods from whom she had received nothing. In this she was different from ordinary harlots who at least asked for hire from their visitors (vs. 34).

Yet, according to the present form of the passage—and here the unconditional grace of God shines forth—all this will be forgiven. Because the love of the Lord is inexhaustible, he will remember the covenant made in her youth and will set up an everlasting covenant with her (vss. 60 ff.). Her only punishment will be that, in seeing the grace of the Lord, she will be put to shame. She must experience the humiliation brought about by unconditional love in spite of the basest sins. Hopefully, this will prevent her from ever being adulterous again. She will not follow the ways of her past but will remember and be confounded, and never open your mouth again because of your shame, when I forgive you all that you have done, says the Lord GOD (vs. 63).

Indeed, there are few passages in the Bible which proclaim more forcefully the unconditional divine grace.

Another passage in Ezekiel to be considered is 20:1-44. In it the in-spite-of form appears once again. There are altogether four rebellious periods mentioned in the past, to three of which the Lord responded with forgiveness. The periods were the time spent in Egypt, the time of the wilderness wanderings, the time of the first generation after the conquest,[4] and the time of the post-conquest fathers (vss. 7, 13, 18, 27). Three times the sins were forgiven because, as the Lord said, "I acted for the sake of my name" (vss. 9, 14, 22); as it is assumed, only the fourth time were the sins punished by the exile. The reason for forgiveness is a well-known motif in Ezekiel and means that by losing his "name," i.e., fame, the Lord would lose his hold on the nations.[5] At any rate, the point is that at no time did Israel deserve forgiveness.

The fifth case was the rebellion of the prophet's own generation. What their sin was is impossible to see clearly. According to vss. 1 ff., the elders came to Ezekiel to inquire for something, and that inquiry had to do with sin.[6] Judging from vss. 32 ff., which refer to the tradition in 1 Samuel 8:7 ff., 12:17b, i.e., to Israel's rebellion against the Lord in requesting a king, the sin was the intention to elect a political leader, perhaps one of the descendants of David. The response of the Lord to this sin and, of course, to the sin resulting in the captivity, will be the restoration of the cult in Jerusalem and the gathering of the people to the land of Israel but without a Davidic king (vs. 33b).

The message of the chapter is the same as that of chapter 16 and of the rebellion stories in the Tetrateuch: Despite repeated rebellions God forgives. The history, the life of

Israel, never rested on Israel's obedience, national strength, or political wisdom. It rested on the pure grace of God. The history of salvation is not a series of human achievements but a series of forgiving divine acts. The result of the most recent forgiving act, the prophet hopes, will be that Israel will not walk any more in the ways of the fathers, either of the generation of Egypt, the generation of the conquest, of the post-conquest fathers, or of the generation just preceding the exile. That is, the reference to the negative archetypes, the rebellious fathers, and the proclamation of the divine grace once again serve the purpose of warning the generation of the exile to be loyal henceforth to the Lord.

> . . . you shall remember your ways and all the doings with which you have polluted yourselves; and you shall loathe yourselves for all the evils that you have committed. And you shall know that I am the LORD, when I deal with you for my name's sake, not according to your evil ways, nor according to your corrupt doings (20:43 f.).

The first of the Psalms using the in-spite-of form is Psalm 78. It is a "wisdom Psalm," a didactic poem reflecting great learning,[7] as its introduction, characteristic of wisdom instructions, shows (cf. Prov. 3:1; 4:1; 5:1, etc.). As it stands now, it is probably post-exilic, of about the same age as the Tetrateuch, but since it assumes that God had "rejected the tent of Joseph, he did not choose the tribe of Ephraim" (vs. 67) and that Jerusalem and the Davidic dynasty are still standing, its main body is pre-exilic.

In proclaiming the divine grace it mentions all rebellion stories of the Tetrateuch (water from the rock, vs. 15; quails, manna, vss. 19-29; fiery serpents, vss. 33 ff.; Baal-Peor, vs. 37)[8] and refers also to the post-conquest fathers (vss. 56 ff.). In mentioning the rebellions it refers over and over again to the gracious responses of the Lord in saving acts. There were four, perhaps five, such responses. First was the giving of water from the rock; second, pouring manna from heaven and send-

ing the quails; third—as it seems—sparing the people after
the sin of the spies; fourth, the deliverance from the Philistine
threat; and fifth, the establishment of Jerusalem as the city of
the sanctuary and of the Davidic dynasty as the legitimate
royal house of Israel (vss. 15, 23, 38, 66, 68-70). The proclamation of grace is summarized in vs. 38:

> Yet he, being compassionate,
>   forgave their iniquity,
>   and did not destroy them;
> he restrained his anger often,
>   and did not stir up all his wrath.

Thus, in proclaiming God's forgiveness of rebellions, the
in-spite-of form of the negative archetype of the fathers emerges
clearly, yet the main purpose of the psalmist was didactic, i.e.,
he underlined the positive archetypes given in the divine commandments:

> He established a testimony in Jacob,
>   and appointed a law in Israel,
> which he commanded our fathers
>   to teach to their children;
>   . . . so that they should set their hope in God,
> and not forget the works of God,
>   but keep his commandments;
> and that they should not be like their fathers,
>   a stubborn and rebellious generation,
> a generation whose heart was not steadfast,
>   whose spirit was not faithful to God (vss. 5, 7-8).

The other Psalm employing the motif is Psalm 106. Its age
is difficult to determine, but there are indications of pre-exilic
origin. It is familiar with the story of Dathan and Abiram but
without the certainly post-exilic element of Korah the Levite's
rebellion (vss. 16 ff.). In vs. 5 the collective "I" appears,
reminding one of the king. Yet, in speaking about captives and
asking to "gather us from among the nations," it seems to imply
the Babylonian captivity. Thus a post-exilic origin is also
possible.

Whatever the age of the Psalm may be, it is not praise as

its initial words may indicate, but a Psalm of supplication recited for the purpose expressed in vs. 47:

> Save us, O LORD our God,
>> and gather us from among the nations,
> that we may give thanks to thy holy name
>> and glory in thy praise.

The specific prayer form that it uses shows beyond doubt that it is a supplication. The form is what students of comparative religion call "magical antecedent,"[9] which in biblical interpretation we may call *antecedent of salvation*. Such antecedents were intended to strengthen the effectiveness of a prayer and consisted of mentioning previous saving interventions of the Lord for the purpose of moving him to do the same that he did once upon a time (cf. Pss. 5:4, 12; 10:17; 32:11; 55:22; 139:19; 146:8, etc.).

The Psalm in its entirety is such an antecedent of salvation. It mentions the negative archetype of the fathers at the Sea, the quails, Dathan and Abiram, the golden calf, the spies, Baal-Peor, Meribah, the sins of the post-conquest fathers, the idolatries under the judges and the kings (vss. 7, 17, 19, 28, 34 ff.), and the gracious responses of the Lord to all these rebellions (vss. 8 ff., 15a, 23, 30, 44). We may find his point in reminding the Lord of what he did in the past in vs. 45:

> He remembered for their sake his covenant,
>> and relented according to the abundance of his
>>> steadfast love.

In other words, as an "antecedent of salvation," the Psalm asks that as the Lord has forgiven the rebellions of the past and brought salvation, so may he do now. The didactic purpose is also present. As the negative archetypes are mentioned and the saving acts of God are recited as antecedents of salvation, it is also implied tacitly that the generation for which the prayer is spoken should not and will not rebel.

The last passage to be analyzed is in the work of the Chronicler. As the text stands now, the motif is part of the description of a great celebration (Neh. 9-10) by which, as the Chronicler believed, "Israel" was restored after the exile, that is, the Jerusalem community was established. The passage in the two chapters bears traces of conscious "scholarly" construction. The material is not uniform, yet everything is carefully and impressively put together. In its present form the description follows the pattern of the covenant repetitions in the Deuteronomic History, and, according to the Chronicler, it is the most important of all such repetitions.[10] In Hebrew it is not called a covenant but rather a "contract" or "an agreement to be kept loyally" (*amanah*; 9:38), yet the author ascribed to it, doubtless, the significance of a covenant. The reason he did not use the word equivalent in Hebrew to "covenant" (*berith*) was that, as he believed, real covenants were only the one at Sinai and those which were mentioned in the Deuteronomic History.[11]

The solemnity and importance of this covenant repetition is underlined by him, a man of scribal accuracy, by the fact that it was written down in a document (9:38) and sealed by the participants. By and large the solemn ceremony follows the pattern of the *word covenants* of the Old Testament which, in turn, were an abbreviated form of the ancient Near Eastern covenants.[12] As the covenant of Moab (Deut. 29:1), it has, first, the recitation of God's mighty acts; second, a curse and an oath; and third, the stipulations. The first element is in the prayer, ascribed to Ezra by the Greek; the second is mentioned, but not quoted, in 10:29; and the third is represented by the sevenfold obligation laid upon themselves by the covenanting congregation in 10:30-39.[13]

The motif of the rebellions and God's gracious responses to them is found in the first section. Following the outline of the Tetrateuch and of the Deuteronomic History, both known in some form to its author, the prayer mentions the creation, the covenant with Abraham, the deliverance from Egypt, the covenant at Sinai, the giving of the law, the manna, and water from the rock. The first rebellion appears as the appointment of a leader to take the people back to Egypt,[14] to which the Lord responded with forgiveness. The second rebellion was the golden calf, which was forgiven likewise, and as a result, the Lord led the people with the pillar of fire and cloud, gave his "good Spirit to instruct them" (9:20; a tradition not known to the Tetrateuch either), provided for them, and conquered the land for them. The third rebellion, says the prayer, took place in the land, under the judges, in the form of "blasphemies" (vs. 26), i.e., idolatries. It was punished but then forgiven. In spite of warnings by the prophets, the last rebellion was under the monarchies, during the "many years." It was eventually punished by giving the people "into the hand of the peoples of the lands" (vs. 30). Proof that it was also forgiven is, however, as the prayer believes, that the returnees are here. Then we read that the restoration is not as yet perfect; "Israel" is not yet free because she lives under foreign domination. Therefore, in order that God may show his goodwill fully, a covenant is made, as described in chapter 10.

From all this, the meaning and function of the prayer is clear. Being the preamble to a covenant, it mentions first the gracious acts of the Lord by which he laid the foundations of Israel (creation and Abraham), and then it tells about the second group of the Lord's good deeds, his saving acts in Egypt, in the wilderness, before the captivity, and his bringing the deportees home. This second group, however, is not only part of a preamble but its members serve also as "antecedents of salvation" in the meaning explained above. Finally, the negative archetypes, the rebellious fathers, are in the service of the author's didactic purpose. This finds expression in two ways: first, in the admission at the end of the prayer that "thou hast dealt faithfully and we have acted wickedly" (9:33b); second, in the sevenfold obligation in 10:30 ff. From now on, therefore, there will be no rebellion in Israel. The people vow

> to walk in God's law which was given by Moses the servant of God, and to observe and do all the commandments of the LORD our Lord and his ordinances and his statutes (10:29).

In conclusion, let it be stated again that the motif of the rebellious fathers appears, indeed, in the great works and the prophetic collections of the Old Testament. It is found in various forms: as *pure negative archetype*, saying, do not do as the fathers did, and as a *charge* that the people are doing as the fathers did; then it appears as part of *confessions of sins,* as the *rebellious history* of Israel, and in *antecedents of salvation.* In all cases it serves a didactic purpose in sounding the warning not to act as the fathers did. In its most complete form, the *in-spite-of* form, it proclaims the unconditional divine grace. If, therefore, such a rich and many-sided use of the motif was possible through many centuries, especially in the centuries not far from the age of the Tetrateuch, the assumption is justified that in using the motif, the purpose of the Tetrateuch was the same or very similar to the purpose of other biblical passages. The purpose was to teach, to warn, and to encourage. And, since the Tetrateuch was written in order to give a program to restored Israel, it can also be concluded that the generation addressed by the motif was post-exilic Judaism.

One final remark, as far as the Old Testament is concerned, may be made. As we have seen, the motif originated, or rather re-emerged, and was strengthened in the North during and after the period of the Canaanite resurgence under the Omrides. But was the attitude of looking at history as a series of rebellions against God born there? Very probably it was not. If it is true —as most scholars believe—that the Yahwist tradition had its roots in the South, then this attitude also had its roots there.

Except for some P additions the pericope in Genesis 2:4—12:3 comes from the Yahwist and knows of four rebellions, four falls, not of Israel but of mankind—the fall of Eve and Adam, of Cain, the sin of the sons of God and the daughters of man, and the tower of Babel (Gen. 3:1 ff.; 4:1 ff.; 6:1 ff.; 11:1 ff.), none of which was, however, followed by total divine destruction. It was, therefore, the Yahwist who, in using fragmentary myths, initiated the motif of the negative archetypes in both aspects: as the presentation of bad examples and as the demonstration of God's forgiveness—except that he did not speak of Israel alone but of mankind as a whole.

Our analysis of the motif of the fathers' rebellions and God's gracious response to them would be incomplete without casting a glance on its occurrences in some representatives of the post-Old Testament literature, the Apocrypha, the Dead Sea Scriptures, and the New Testament.

Since the Apocrypha are all late, written after the present Old Testament was just about completed, they either do not bring anything new or change the meaning of the motif. Thus the books of Esdras, being nothing but an abbreviation of the work of the Chronicler, reproduce almost verbatim the prayer of Ezra in Ezra 9:7 ff. without changing the context or the meaning (1 Esd. 8:76 ff.). The same is the case in Tobit 1:10, where in making a confession Tobit acknowledges that the exile came upon Israel because of the fathers. The motif is changed in a rather strange fashion in the book of Judith. In Achior's speech it is admitted that Israel was brought to captivity because of the fathers' sins, but it also says that if there is no disobedience to the law, God protects her and she is invincible (Jth. 5:17 ff.). This principle gives basis to the curious war plan suggested by Judith which, as the book believes, would have been successful if the condition for it could have been created. The condition was to force the Israelites, by blockading the city of Bethulia, to eat the tithe due the priests. If they did this, Judith says, it would be disobedience to the law; consequently, God would forsake them and they would lose their invincibility (11:10 ff.). That is, while it is fully acknowledged that the captivity was a punishment for the sins of the fathers and that unconditional obedience is now required, the element of divine forgiveness disappears completely.

Also in other Apocryphal books the motif loses its depth and teaches the simple moral that the good are helped and rewarded and the wicked punished. The Wisdom of Solomon implies that only the "rabble" died when punishment came after the miracle of the quails (Wisd. of Sol. 16:2 ff.; cf. Num. 11:33), and that only those were killed by the fiery serpents who did not listen to the commandments of the law and did not trust the Lord (Wisd. of Sol. 16:5-10; cf. Num. 21:9). The motif appears in almost the same simplicity in the book of Baruch. In his long prayer, full of echoes of Old Testament confessions of sins and of other passages, Baruch admits that the captivity was a divine punishment for the fathers' sins; but it is also said that the generation of the exile is now just about perfect (1:16 ff.; 3:7). That is, the book believes that the restoration did not come by grace but as a reward.

In quoting the sin of Dathan, Abiram, and Korah, both the Wisdom of Solomon and Ecclesiasticus explain the story according to its meaning in the Tetrateuch, but they sharpen its point. The first tells that Aaron was a faultless man and delights in the fact that his service was effective in stopping the plague (Wisd. of Sol. 18:21 ff.). The second, after telling the story, enumerates the privileges of the priesthood (Ecclus. 45:18 ff.).

The Dead Sea Scriptures have a similar tendency to what we have found in the Wisdom of Solomon and Baruch, yet, in accordance with the belief of the sect that they alone represented true Israel, a change is made. In the liturgy of initiation (or more probably in the liturgy of the yearly repetition of the covenant), the motif is present in reference to Psalm 106. The rebellions of the fathers and the mercy of God are mentioned, and it is implied that to those who had joined the sect, the rebellions of the fathers and their own sins were forgiven (Gaster, p. 40).[15] In the Zadokite Document—very much in the fashion of St. Augustine's heavenly and earthly cities— a parallel is drawn between those who have rebelled against God and those who have obeyed him since ancient times. The fallen angels, the giants, the generation of the flood, the sons of Jacob, the rebellions in the wilderness, and the evil kings are mentioned on one side; Noah, Abraham, and Jacob on the other side. The conclusion is made that, even though they were within the covenant, the sinners always perished. The point is the same as in the above-mentioned liturgy: Only those who are members of the sect are the true people of God; the rest of the Jews, although within the covenant, will perish (Gaster, p. 65).

The same dualism, the confrontation of the sinners and the obedient of ancient times, can be observed in one of the psalms of the sect where the conclusion is drawn that God always saved the faithful. The moral is also the same: The members of the community are forgiven; the rest of mankind, or of Israel, is lost (Gaster, p. 197). In the Book of the War, the rebellion of Nadab and Abihu is mentioned but its point is changed. The point here is to remind those who showed weakness in the battle that these two sons of Aaron were punished, while the other two, Eleazar and Ithamar, were rewarded. Although the premise is somewhat awkward, this conclusion can be drawn: Fight on and be rewarded as Eleazar and Ithamar were.

In the New Testament the motif appears in three forms. In the Gospel of John (3:14) the "lifting up" of Christ, the Son of Man who came from heaven, i.e., his departure from earth, is compared with the lifting up of the bronze serpent in the wilderness by Moses (cf. John 8:28; 12:32). Here the story is interpreted as in the Wisdom of Solomon, and the underlying attitude is that of the Qumran sect. The message is this: Now is the time; a decision must be made. As at that time those who looked upon the serpent were healed; now those who believe in the lifted-up Son of Man will have eternal life. John, however, gives a different interpretation of the serpent as a symbol. According to the Wisdom of Solomon, those who looked upon the serpent actually made a decision for the law and so were saved; at this time not the serpent, not the law, is lifted up, but Christ. He who decides for him in believing that he is indeed the heavenly Son of Man belongs to the "sons of light" (John 12:36), to the company of Jesus, i.e., as in Qumran, to the new people of God, and is saved not for physical but eternal life.

The same form is found in the Letter to the Hebrews (3:1—4:13). It also calls for a decision except that the author is more definite. He refers to Psalm 95:8-11. That Psalm reminds its audience of Massah and Meribah, and using the story as a negative archetype, asks that they not do as the fathers did but return to the Lord. The author of the Letter to the Hebrews issues the same call and warns against imitating the rebellious generation. But he goes one step further. In referring to the story of the spies, he states that the wilderness generation did not enter the rest of God, i.e., Canaan, offered to them (4:2 ff.); therefore, an invitation to enter the rest of God was once again issued through Christ. To strengthen his point he makes a play on words (*sabbath* means "rest"), and says that those who accept the invitation will receive eternal rest, i.e., participate in the eternal sabbath. The message is the same as in John: Now is the time for a decision. In Christ a new opportunity is offered. Those who believe in him will enter the eternal rest; they will belong to the new people of God.

The second form of the motif in the New Testament is

the rebellious history. It is found in Matthew 23:29 ff., its parallel, Luke 11:45 ff., and in Stephen's speech in Acts 7. In the Gospels no wilderness rebellion is mentioned but reference is made to the "prophets" from Abel to Zechariah the son of Barachiah (confused with the son of Jehoiada of 2 Chronicles 24:20) who, according to the charge, were killed by the rebellious people of Israel. As is well known, Stephen's speech also views the history of Israel as continuous rebellion. It tells that history, beginning with the first rebels, the sons of Jacob (Acts 7:9), goes on telling about the quarreling Israelites who refused Moses' mediation in Egypt, and mentions the golden calf and, finally, the building of the temple by Solomon which, according to Stephen, was the worst rebellion (vss. 26 ff., 35, 39 ff., 47 ff.). Then he concludes:

> You stiff-necked people, uncircumcised in heart and ears, you always resist the Holy Spirit. As your fathers did, so do you. Which of the prophets did not your fathers persecute? And they killed those who announced beforehand the coming of the Righteous One, whom you have now betrayed and murdered, you who received the law as delivered by angels and did not keep it (vss. 51-53).

Thus the aim of the speech is to warn Israel not to do as the fathers did in rebelling against God and refusing him, but to accept the gospel. Cease to be the rebellious people of God, and in accepting Jesus, change to be his obedient children.

The third form of the motif is found in Paul (1 Cor. 10: 1-13). He mentions the events of the exodus, then instances of rebellions, the manna and the rock (vss. 1-5), the golden calf, Baal-Peor, the serpents, and the murmuring of the people after the destruction of Korah and his companions (vss. 7-10). But he makes use of the motif not for missionary purposes, as the three other writers did, but for the purpose of instruction (i.e., not for the purpose of *kerygma* but for *didachē*). He addresses the Corinthians, who are already Christians, and warns them not to follow the bad example of the fathers in worshiping idols. Thus he remains faithful to the original intention of the motif in the Tetrateuch and elsewhere in the Old Testament.

Yet there is a difference. In agreement with the Apocryphal wisdom literature (Wisdom of Solomon, Ecclesiasticus) and the Essenes, Paul believes that only some members of Israel rebelled at various occasions and only the guilty were punished. He makes this point in every case. Since the order of the stories is different in his passage and he changes the twenty-four thousand of Numbers 25:9 to twenty-three thousand (vs. 8), it is obvious that the quotations were made from memory. His context is strictly Christian. He identifies the Rock (which according to rabbinic tradition followed the people in the wilderness and supplied water all the time) with Christ and believes that the water and the manna were heavenly food and drink (Ps. 78:25). Since, like all Christians, he believed that the church was the eschatological Israel, the people of God "upon whom the end of the ages has come," he thinks that the rebellion stories were written down for the benefit of his generation that they may learn and may not act as the rebellious fathers did (vs. 11). This is, then, why he adds to the stories warnings against idolatry (vss. 14-33).

6
THE SIGNIFICANCE OF THE REBELLION MOTIF FOR THE NEW ISRAEL

If the patient reader who has read all that has gone before is a biblical scholar, he may have found a few things interesting, others just repetitions of what has already been said by others, and he may have agreed or disagreed with what he has read. On the other hand, if he is a man (or woman) without formal training in biblical scholarship, he may have found some passages boring and it may seem difficult for him to see what all this has to do with the church. But if what has been said has no relevance for the church and the Christian faith, writing it down was absolutely useless and reading it was a waste of time. The writer, therefore, feels that it is necessary to justify what he has written by pointing out briefly its possible significance for the church.

First let us summarize what has been said. Its essence was that from the ninth century on, perhaps even before that, it had become something of a habit in Israel to survey the past of the nation and discover and condemn the sins of the fathers. As a result, two kinds of sins became clear. One was disloyalty to the Lord, and the other lack of confidence in his saving will and power. Those who did the survey—first, the faithful depositories of the traditions, the tribes of the old confederacy; then, the prophets—proclaimed that responsibility for the sins of the fathers must be accepted, and that the miseries which befell Israel from generation to generation were the just punishment of the Lord. But they were not merely condemning. They held up the bad example of the fathers in order that the sons would not commit the same sins again, and from now on (and this "now" was always the age of the particular generation doing the survey) Israel would keep the covenant and all that went with it. Finally, the proclamation of God's grace was also part of their message. They said that in spite of the sins of the past, and of the present, that grace was still available. The sins were forgiven because the Lord would never utterly reject his people. He had set up a plan of salvation and would bring it to its end, even with all human will to the contrary, and against all resistance. Each generation heard, therefore, in their own particular "now," that they might look forward with confidence and be open and willing to accept God's grace.

That this message is for the Christian church is to be emphatically affirmed. That is, it does not have the same significance, and certainly not the same meaning, for the Jewish community. What it means for them is not the business of the present writer. He speaks exclusively within the Christian church and, if he may, asks for a hearing only on the part of the church. He is fully aware of the fundamental difference between Old Israel and New Israel, a difference which cannot, and should not, be explained away by superficial humanism. That difference is the self-understanding of Judaism and of the church. Both understand themselves as the true Israel, the direct continuation of God's people. The Jew could never resign this claim (and the present writer would have little respect for a Jew who would do that), but neither can the church do it. If the Jew resigned his claim, he would cease to be a Jew; if the church did it, her existence would be meaningless. Of course, the church must admit that Judaism is and will always be God's people in a peculiar manner, yet not in the way Israel was. This has to be said here because the writer has respected Jewish friends and it would be painful for him if they misunderstood him.

What is that message, then, for the church? One might

answer that the message is given in the interpretations of Matthew, Luke, John, the Letter to the Hebrews, and Paul. But these writers do not interpret the motif according to its original intentions. With his didactic tendency, Paul comes closest to it, yet he too makes changes. Those who use the motif as part of the proclamation believe that the first invitation to enter the "rest of God," i.e., to be his people, was not accepted by the wilderness generation, and now, with the appearance of Jesus, a new invitation has been issued comparable to the first yet overriding it. Over against the Old Testament, this interpretation is new; it is the missionary call, which, of course, is still to be issued, yet it is not in line with the original context. Paul also changes the meaning of the motif. He removes the responsibility from the people of God as a whole and lets only the "wicked" be punished. Besides, he speaks through it only to the Christians.

This motif should not be understood as a discovery of the "doctrine of original sin" in the Old Testament.[1] The doctrine of original sin (for the sake of clarity, this non-biblical term must be used here) in its Pauline meaning is not found in the Old Testament, and for that matter neither is it found in the New Testament outside of Paul. As is well known, it has to do with Adam as not only the ancestor but also the "root of mankind"[2] and is built on the idea known to comparative religion as the corporate body. This holds that the root, the forefather, stands for all descendants, and whatever was true and valid for him is true and valid for the entire corporate body existing now. Paul (particularly in Rom. 1:18—3:20) explains the hopeless corruption of mankind, both Jews and Gentiles, by means of the corporate body of Adam and holds that no man can leave that body by his own effort. In the rebellion motif, the idea of the corporate body plays no important part. It appears only in the belief that responsibility for the fathers' sins must be accepted by the sons. Yet the fathers sinned not because they were corrupt inherently, but because they chose rebellion deliberately, and if the sons followed the example of their fathers, they did so either because they were taught so or because of habit which, if they had wished, could have been resisted or broken.

The message of the motif should be heard in its original meaning, a meaning which is not known in the New Testament. As has been shown, the attitude suggested by the motif was to look back through the centuries and admit that the history of God's people (in the Christian context, the history of the church) was a series of rebellions against God. This is its point in the Old Testament, particularly in the form of rebellious history, and this is the point of Stephen's speech in the book of Acts. True, one aspect of the biblical story is that the history of God's people consists of his saving "mighty acts," which certainly cannot be ignored; yet these acts should always be viewed from the opposite side, against the background of human rebellions. The contribution of man to the biblical story, and for that matter to the history of the church, was not positive or promoting, but negative and destructive. What has been achieved by any one generation was due not to man but to God.

This human side of the biblical story, and of the church as history, could not be seen clearly by the church during the short period of the apostolic age and, indeed, she had little time to rebel against the new and decisive act of forgiveness of God. The first Christians were intoxicated by the overwhelming joy of God's appearance in Christ and by the hope of his early return. Thus the New Testament writers did not deal with the problem of the church's past sins. This is not to say that they were not familiar with the rebellious attitude of man; they do occasionally point out the sins of the church, e.g., Paul's condemnation of the Corinthians, or in the book of Revelation, Christ's condemnation of the sins of at least six of his seven churches. The message of the rebellions is, therefore, not a particularly New Testament message. Yet, it can hardly be denied that it is in perfect agreement with the general New Testament attitude. At any rate, it is certainly a biblical message, and if the Old Testament belongs to the church as the New Israel, the message must be heard by her.

Perhaps listening to it is distressing. Just as no human group would be glad to discover that its past was crude and barbaric, no religious group would be enthusiastic if told that its past contained nothing but a continual rejection of that particular reality, the divine, by which and for which it existed. Seen from the side of man, the church is also a human religious group, and it takes courage, as it did for the Old Testament people of God, to accept the message in humility, or to use a familiar phrase, in fear and trembling. No doubt, the church did and does know about her past, and she does discover and admit rebellions in it. Yet we are inclined to condemn "them," that is, certain parties in the church, and not our own group. No better example can be quoted of this than the case of the Reformation which, as a rule, is interpreted in an extreme way by the parties concerned, and only most recently have voices been heard from both camps that somehow and in some way "we" are also guilty in the disruption of the church. Yet, even in admitting the "we" are not always beyond reproof either, we try to minimize the case by saying that the fathers were not really rebellious but only made a "mistake." That is, the repentant, the broken, attitude of Ezra or Nehemiah is not known or is not welcome to us.

But why should the church listen to this message? After all, it is "only" an Old Testament message, or to use a term of comparative religion, it is only an element of the numinous experience of a long-past religious community, the condemnation of the past representing the "creature feeling," the negative, the fearful pole of the "holy," while hope in the divine grace represents its positive pole, the attractive, the fascinating.[3] In answering the question, something must be mentioned, something that has been sounded in all generations of the church, something that in some ages had been listened to by many, but never by all, and which so many times went unheard. This is that the church's foundation is the Word become not only flesh but also Scripture, that she is built on the foundation of the prophets and apostles. In our case, of course, the prophets should be underlined.

Of course, the statement that the church stands under the supreme authority of the Word as it appears, for the age after Christ, in Scripture, asks for a "prejudiced" mind. Yet, if the church is indeed the church of Jesus Christ, no other way is possible for her. In the moment this "prejudice" is relinquished, the church becomes nothing more than a religious society and the Christian individual a mere religious man. For the problem is not whether the church is a useful, a respectable, organization, whether its members are people assuming responsibility for all that is good, whether they are willing to take heroic actions for the improvement of the individual and of society, or whether her beliefs are acceptable to the world, poor and rich, sophisticated scholars and the less educated. The problem is rather whether she is *Christian,* that is, whether she accepts fully and unconditionally the supreme authority of her Lord as witnessed in Scripture. This "prejudice" implies the full realization of the church's unique, strange—and let us admit—embarrassing, situation, which is that she is the only human organization which does not live in the world from the immanent, but from above, from the transcendent.

The acceptance of this status means that when the church searches for fellowship with the divine, for "redemption from the evanescent"[4] in Christian terms, for salvation and for the means by which that salvation comes, she does not turn to the respectable realms of philosophy, psychology of religion, or the fascinating discipline of comparative religion, but simply, one-sidedly, and with a childlike attitude, she turns to Scripture. It means that the church is willing to accept as her only task the full and unconditional serving of the world—that world which the Father of Jesus Christ loved—and proclaims and mediates salvation to that world. It means that in her faith and acts the church listens to the Word. This proclamation, mediation, and service ought not—nor can it—begin with a careful survey of the given human or social situation, with an examination of man's predicament, a collection of statistical data, or the preparation of a well-laid-out plan, and then search for the medicines to be applied, even though the greater part of those medicines might be drawn from Christian "principles." The first thing the church ought to do is to receive the command from above, regardless of the given situation, and then proceed, perhaps, with examining the human situation, the statistical data, and the planning.

Yet always the command, a firm standing on the Word, is the primary base, not the given situation. The church's task is not to supply the best or most workable ideology, the best faith men can live by; neither is her primary task to reform society. Her primary task is to proclaim and bring salvation to the world through Christ. Of course, the church, the City of God, may and should cooperate with the world, the Earthly City, as far as human tranquillity and order are concerned;[5] that is, she may—why not, after all?—develop an ideology, take part in social reform, and even enjoy the fun of philosophizing.[6] But as the church of Christ, she may do all this only in order that her primary task, the bringing of salvation, be made easier and her message be more readily heard. Any philosophical pursuit, any scholarly work, and any social endeavor which does not serve this end in the church should be considered as disloyalty and rebellion against her Lord. To the charge that this is prejudice and narrow-mindedness, the church's answer can be given by the alleged statement of Luther's, "My conscience is taken captive by God's Word. . . . On this I take my stand. I can do no other. God help me."

Keeping all this in mind, perhaps a few concrete examples may be mentioned here. The first may be the rebellion, which, in our higher culture trained in philosophical thought, is one of the most common rebellions. The term *liberal theology* may be a convenient name, but nowadays it is used vaguely and many times covers ventures which have little to do with what is meant here. It is better, therefore, to call it *philosophical theology,* a term which came into vogue recently and adequately covers the meaning. At any rate, a characteristic of this kind of thinking is that when the affair of Christian faith and truth is under discussion, the point of departure is not Scripture but the free observation of man's environment, his situation within it, his existential or religious experience, and the like. It is based on contemplation free from the Word of God, as the individual thinker sees fit. It may appear as philosophy or psychology of religion; it may follow the line of a special inner experience, and is sometimes called constructive theology. Of course, if he who is engaged in its pursuit happens to have, among other things, a Christian background—and he may even be a professor at a seminary— he will use Christian terms which, however, serve only as illustrations of the philosophical results already achieved and have little to do with the use of the terms in their biblical context.

To deal with the problem of philosophical theology extensively and in the depth it deserves would demand a long essay. Only this much can be said here—that this kind of mental activity is ancient in the church. It appeared as soon as Christianity entered the Hellenistic world and men of education accepted the gospel, men who, due to the divergence of biblical and Greek philosophical modes of thinking, were unable to understand the peculiar thought forms of the Bible. These men, driven by the otherwise respectable intention to express the Christian truth in a language understandable to themselves and to their colleagues, interpreted the Christian message as the "true philosophy" and presented it in the thought forms of Hellenistic philosophy. It is enough to recall here Justin Martyr of the second century, who was the first to begin speaking about the preexistent Christ as the container of the Neoplatonic ideas, the eternal patterns, or Augustine, for whom—according to one line of his thought, the Neoplatonic —the "folly" and the "stumbling block" of the cross were removed, because Christ served as mere bait set by God for man to free himself from his sin, i.e., his misdirected love, and to redirect it toward God.[7]

Or what shall we say about Thomas Aquinas, the prince of the Scholastics? He was certainly a Christian, but if one considers only his Aristotelian-Platonic side, his God, in spite of the awesome beauty of his system, is little more than a cosmic force for which, with some changes, could be easily substituted the nuclear energy of modern physics. To their credit, however, it must be said that these fathers of the church, in meeting some elements of the Christian truth difficult to express or explain by means of Hellenistic philosophy, had the courage to side with the Christian truth and not vice versa. Contact with the Christian background was broken only by the Renaissance and Baroque philosophers, and after that time it became fashionable to use Christian images only as illustrations or labels for ideas totally alien to the Bible (e.g., Joachim of Floris, Pico della Mirandola, Giordano Bruno, Michael Servetus, Faustus Socinus, Boehme, Spinoza).

Paradoxically, the first who began to put up resistance to the endeavor to grasp the truly divine without biblical revelation was the "skeptic" and "atheist" Hume, and after him

Kant. The former courageously declared that those who defend the Christian religion by the principles of human reason are either its "dangerous friends or disguised enemies." He was not afraid to say that "to be a philosophical skeptic is . . . the first and most essential step towards being a believing Christian."[8] The latter, as is well known, said that the "noumenon" of God is merely a projection of the human mind itself which transforms the subjective conditions of our thinking into objective conditions of objects themselves.[9] Yet philosophical theologians did not listen to their voices. As the result of the shock caused by the scientific and historical situation of the nineteenth century, we again find thinkers who retained some of the biblical truth but mixed it with philosophy or "experience" (Schleiermacher, Ritschl) or who followed the way of pure philosophical theology (Hegel, Marx). But with this, we come to our own age, and perhaps the best way to illustrate the kind of rebellion that took place against the Word is to refer to John Oman, a theologian of the first half of this century who deserves much more attention than he usually receives.[10]

What is the essence of his system? Having little to do with Christianity, his thoughts are mainly based on his own observations and contemplation, but he acknowledges his indebtedness to other philosophical theologians. His general tendency is Platonic, but he also borrowed much from Spinoza, Schleiermacher, Hegel, Ritschl, Windelband, Kant, and many others, and yet, strictly speaking, he is not a disciple of any of them. It is difficult to classify him according to accepted categories. He is a pantheist, a panentheist, but not in the usual sense. Perhaps the term "hylozoism" of the pre-Socratic philosophers comes closest to his system, but even that is not fully adequate. Since in his book he put together a tremendous amount of learning, yet nowhere does he give a systematic presentation of his own results, the best method to present his views in an unjustly abbreviated form is to ask three questions: What is the divine for man? How can man know and come in contact with it? What is the result if this knowledge and contact are established?

What is the divine? According to Oman it is man's environment (p. 212) in a qualified sense. He distinguishes two aspects of this environment: One appears to sensation as the Natural, the other as the Supernatural, when that environment is valued as such. The two aspects belong inseparably together. The Natural mirrors the Supernatural (p. 169), and the Supernatural manifests itself through the Natural (p. 205). The Natural is the world which surrounds us, but, as the Supernatural, it manifests more than natural values, and demands to be esteemed as sacred (pp. 205 f.). Not being in opposition, the two aspects are continuously interwoven so that nothing can be wholly natural or wholly supernatural. Being a reality in the true sense of the word, the Supernatural can be experienced just as well as the Natural, and it appeals to and has the same authority for experience as the Natural (p. 101, cf. 97). It is, therefore, its own sole witness (p. 208). Since the Supernatural manifests itself through the Natural, it can be reached by man. Even more, if the Supernatural is not manifested by the Natural it is not truly Supernatural; and the Natural, if it is not the manifestation of the Supernatural, but only physical, is not truly the Natural (p. 205). We experience the same one reality as partly natural, the values of which are relative and serve our needs, and partly as supernatural, the values of which are absolute, to which our needs must submit (p. 72).

To our second question, "How can man know the Supernatural and how can he come in contact with it," Oman answers that this can be accomplished by discovering the absolute values of the Supernatural through the Natural. Higher values can already be discerned in the Natural; they are the values of Plato—beauty, goodness, and truth. The Supernatural stands above them. In determining the means by which we discover it, Oman makes use of the idea of the holy, relying, however, more on Windelband than on Otto (pp. 60 ff., 474), and says that man first experiences the Supernatural as the material holy, which is related to the experience of the beautiful. This, however, is not sufficient because although "holy" is a value judgment, it is still material, not ideal. Only in making the judgment that the Supernatural is sacred, that it has absolute worth, do we begin to know it really (pp. 59, 90). The higher value of the sacred is related to goodness. Finally, when we affirm the reality of the Supernatural, we submit to the absolute truth, and this judgment is akin to the relative truth that can already be experienced in the Natural (pp. 206, 208). Thus, the mere judgment of holy must give place to reverence, the reverence of the sacred, which frees us from the bondage of the Natural (pp. 306, 308). There is, therefore, a continuous climbing upward in knowledge from the Natural to the Supernatural, as on a ladder, by which we come to a finer, more objective sense of the beauty of holiness, to a higher knowledge of the sacred in which we can realize our true empirical selves, and to the recognition that the Supernatural is truly the Father of our spirits who works for a purpose beyond the world (pp. 143, 425 ff.). This upward movement, however, can begin only if we approach the Supernatural in freedom, by our own choice and not as a must; if we are attracted by its vision above us (pp. 294, 309, 311); and if we go upward with higher meaning in front of us and are not pushed by an impact from behind (p. 265).

What is the result of this upward movement, giving us contact with the Supernatural? As Oman believes, its commencement had an important result even for primitive man. Being a child of his age, he accepts the idea of evolution and holds that the experience of the natural holy gave primitive man the first firm foothold in the flux of the senses and with that his evolution as man began. But the Supernatural also acted as a force within the cosmos itself. Evolution of life is like the evolution of man's house, his dwelling, which grew slowly. First it was a dark abode, then it was built higher, life opened its windows to higher meanings, and in our time it reached its present highest point in the citizen of the world (p. 274). This took place because of the existence of the Supernatural as the highest meaning. So life began in slime, yet developed to higher forms because of the meaningful reality above (pp. 279, 293 f.).

Finally, according to Oman, the correct knowledge and service of the Supernatural was achieved by the prophetic religion of the Old Testament and by Jesus. They experienced the reconciliation of the evanescent to the eternal and thereby the eternal was revealed to them (pp. 449, 470). They understood that the world belongs to God, who is the meaning of the evanescent (pp. 447 ff.). They discovered the eternal value of the individual, and that sin is not the breaking of rules but disloyalty to one's own worth (pp. 450, 455); they appreciated that the duty of man is to realize God's final order in the present (p. 446), and learned to live in the concrete environment according to its supernatural meaning and purpose (p. 471).

To give a sound analysis of Oman's system, one which would deal with its merits and faults as it deserves, would take us too far afield. However, it is clear that as far as its basic foundations are concerned, it has nothing to do with biblical thought. It has nothing to do with the belief that the cosmos and man are creatures, that in themselves they are not divine, and that they never coincide with the divine. Neither has it anything in common with the biblical ideas that the divine revealed himself in the world of man at opportunities like

Israel, her cult, Jesus, the church, her proclamation and her sacraments. For Oman, not certain parts of man's world, selected in a sovereign manner by God, are the exclusive points of his self-manifestation, but the entire cosmos. Thus he participates in a rebellion, most repulsive for biblical man, that the natural in its totality may and does reveal the divine. As a modern thinker, unlike the Greeks and the Scholastics, he does not build on observation and reasoning but deals with the problem on the basis of his specific religious experience. He presents his findings as truths, which, apparently, gives him a certain peace of mind. This brings him very close to the Gnostics, for whom "saving knowledge" was vitally important also, and makes one conjecture that what he really experienced was a breakthrough of the unconscious to the conscious, an experience similar to that of the Zen Buddhist as analyzed by C. G. Jung.[11] An analysis of other systems of philosophical theology, e.g., of that of Martin Buber or of the more recent systems of Paul Tillich and Thomas Altizer, would show that what has been said about Oman would also be true, with little change, for them.[12]

By now we may leave this sophisticated form of rebellion and turn to orthodoxy, called in its popular and distorted form "fundamentalism." The subject deserves a more profound analysis but our space is limited. The most convenient way seems to be to deal with the small but recent book of E. J. Carnell.[13] Even though Carnell's thought does not represent classical orthodoxy anymore, the most important characteristics are still there.

Carnell touches the essence of orthodoxy in defining it thus: "Orthodoxy is that branch of Christendom which limits the ground of religious authority to the Bible" (p. 13). One would be willing to admit the validity of this statement within the church if both the objective and subjective aspects of the Bible as the ground of revelation were fully seen. But Carnell

stresses one-sidedly the objective aspect. He says that the
Bible possesses divine authority because of its plenary inspiration. In defining "plenary inspiration," he quotes B. B. War-
field, with whom he essentially agrees. "Inspiration is that
extraordinary, supernatural influence (or, passively, the result
of it) exerted by the Holy Ghost on the writers of our Sacred
Books, by which their words were rendered also the words of
God, and, therefore, perfectly infallible" (p. 100). Such being
the case, the words of the Bible have the "force of law" (p.
36). Why should this be admitted? The divine authority of the
Old Testament is not difficult to establish; Christ and the
apostles accepted it. He who would disagree with Christ would
deny his union with the Father, would question his divinity,
and this "would imply *the loss of his Savior*" (pp. 35, 39).
The authority of the New Testament rests on apostolic authority. Either the apostles themselves wrote its books or they
gave them validity, as in the case of Mark and Luke. Therefore, "their canonical authority depends upon their author-
ship" (p. 47). This is true not only for the individual groups
but also for the New Testament canon. "The canon of the
New Testament was decided by the apostles themselves" (p.
45). The apparent inconsistencies between the two Testaments and within the Testaments do not destroy their divine
authority. Certain hermeneutical rules prevent this. For the
Old Testament such rules are the idea of "progressive revelation" and the interpretation of the Old Testament by the New.
As for the New Testament, "the Epistles interpret the
Gospels," the "systematic passages interpret the incidental,"
"universal passages interpret the local," and "didactic passages
interpret the symbolic" (pp. 52 ff.). Finally, Carnell, rather
arbitrarily, decides that should there be any doubt, the Letters
to the Romans and Galatians are to be accepted as final
standards (p. 66).

Why this desperate striving to establish by *historical* and *arbitrary* rules the divine authority of the Bible? Because Carnell shares the basic fear of uncertainty that was behind the emergence and periodic recurrence of the doctrine of verbal, or plenary, inspiration. Fear was in the hearts of the rabbis who created it long before Christianity. They were afraid that without the divine authority of the Old Testament Judaism would disappear in syncretistic Hellenism. In adopting the doctrine from the rabbis, the early church fathers set the "true philosophy" of the inspired Bible against the rival Hellenistic philosophies. The seventeenth century, the age of Protestant high orthodoxy, was a century searching for absolute truths as a response to the Renaissance. This was the century of Descartes, Spinoza, and Leibnitz, men who endeavored to establish mathematical certainty in philosophy. Finally, in the 1920's, it was the challenge of modern science and European modernistic theology that forced the fathers of American fundamentalism to stress verbal inspiration.[14]

Is this doctrine of verbal, or plenary, inspiration a rebellion against the Word? In itself it would not be, but its one-sided emphasis is.[15] How did the New Testament authors write their books? First they were told by the Father that Jesus was the Christ, and then, after this divinely inspired experience (this word "experience," often misused by pietism and liberal theology, can be used safely here), they witnessed to what they had seen and heard (Matt. 16:16 ff.; 1 John 1:1-3). In this sense their writings were, indeed, divinely inspired. This is the truth in orthodoxy's doctrine because this establishes the objective validity of inspiration. But with this, nothing is said as yet about the subjective validity of Scripture. In saying only this much, orthodoxy demonstrated that it did not listen to Paul, who knew that a subjective experience, similar to the experience created by the Spirit in the hearts of the authors, must be created also in the hearts of the readers of the Bible—otherwise its divine authority is null and void. ". . . no one can say 'Jesus is Lord' except by the Holy Spirit" (1 Cor. 12:3). Stressing only the objective side of inspiration, they present us with divinely inspired Scripture as an object of nature from which everything important can be learned about God directly, just as a scientist can gather information about a body tissue under his microscope.

This is nothing less than arresting the divine Word within the human word. Calvin still knew that without a subjective experience nothing can be gained. "It is necessary, therefore, that the same Spirit, who spake by the mouths of the prophets, should penetrate into our hearts, to convince us"; otherwise even the faithful "till he illuminate their minds . . . are perpetually fluctuating amidst a multitude of doubts" (*Institutes,* I.VII.4). Orthodoxy did not see that only those can accept the witness of Scripture who are drawn into the same divine realm in which the prophets and the apostles stood. Carnell seems to know about this,[16] yet he goes on to establish the objective validity of Scripture alone. Such an arresting of the Word within the written word *is* a rebellion because it prevents the free flow of the Spirit. With orthodoxy he is guilty of going to another extreme than experiential-intellectual mythology. He neglects the human experience created by the Spirit when one is faced by Scripture.

Carnell is, however, too much of a scholar to accept fundamentalism, which, incidentally, exists only in this country. He rejects it with strong words and calls it "orthodoxy gone cultic" (pp. 113, 141).[17] He is right except that he does not mention the two other ingredients, radical reformation (the third form of Western Christianity in the sixteenth century besides Romanism and classical reformation) and pietism, both of which were absorbed by fundamentalism with all their virtues and vices. Fundamentalism is probably worse than the other great sect of Christianity, Tridentine Catholicism. The sect is born when it is assumed that man possesses and can express the divine truth. Both these groups make this assumption. There is, however, a difference between the two. In Catholicism this assumption is controlled by high learning, by an honest endeavor to think theologically, and by a tendency toward humanistic culture. We are not concerned here why Catholicism believes to possess the divine truth, but fundamentalism believes it for the same reason as orthodoxy; it also views the Bible as verbally inspired. But hounded by a deeper anxiety than orthodoxy, it goes farther. It is afraid of humanistic culture and embraces obscurantism; erudition may challenge the divine truth. It has legalistic ethics by which, as is believed, perfection can be attained; less than perfection may render the possession of the divine truth questionable. It neglects the sacraments; the sacraments are important only for those who know that they continually need God's renewing power. It prefers separation from historical churches; they tolerate "sinners." Fundamentalism is *hubris,* the rebellious attitude which holds that in the possession of the divine truth man can stand in the place of God.

But dealing with the interpretation of Scripture, one may discover a method which is almost a rebellion or, at least, is harmful for the right understanding of the biblical message. It is found mainly among scholars, and consists in the dangerous practice of presenting certain ancillary disciplines of biblical interpretation as interpretations of faith. It is in vogue today to present archeology, the history of Israel and of the early church, or the literary history of the biblical books for the only "scholarly" forms of biblical interpretation, so that "biblical theology," or rather interpretation, becomes sheer archeology, history, or history of literature. To be sure, it is not denied here that to be thoroughly familiar with the results of these disciplines is absolutely necessary for the biblical interpreter, and that these disciplines should have a respectable place among other forms of systematic knowledge. Yet, obviously, none of them have meaning for the church in themselves. For the church the message, the meaning, is important. The problem, for example, that the Megiddo stables were built by Solomon or Ahab should, indeed, be an important point for archeology, yet for biblical interpretation it is secondary, because these stables speak only about the fact that the people of God appeared, or wanted to appear, rightly or wrongly, as one of the nations. Biblical interpretation cannot be subsumed under its ancillary disciplines. It has to make all possible use of them but never become any one of them.

Rebellions, however, are possible not only philosophically or in approaching and interpreting Scripture, but also in the actions of the church. They have to be placed before the eyes of every generation, regardless of whether those actions took place in the distant past or are taking place in the present. It is impossible to mention all actions of the church which might have been rebellions in the past or may be such today. Only some questions can be asked, similar to those which should be asked over and over again and weighed carefully. Such questions may be: Was it correct for the church to absorb a great deal of Hellenistic culture so that Christianity appeared as a syncretistic religion, or, in order to spread the Christian message, was it inevitable and good? Was the institutionalization of the church during and after the Middle Ages right or wrong? Was the sacramentalism of the church in its Eastern half and in Roman Catholicism correct, or was the almost complete desacramentalization, especially that of modern Protestantism, the right thing to do? Was the restoration of the Middle Ages in Protestant Orthodoxy and the petrification of its ideas in certain confessions acceptable, or is the church better off without clearly defined tenets of faith?

Is it right to create confessions without serious challenge, or should confessions be written only when the church faces mortal threat? Was the attitude of Luther and Calvin that

mission to outsiders is an extraordinary function of the church
and is restricted to some eras admissible? Should the church
require the acceptance of certain elements of Western civilization from young churches, or should it be permitted that the
Christian message create its own cultural body? Was and is
the Constantinian cooperation of the church and state admissible, or should the two be kept completely separate even to
the extent of the atheistic state? Is it a must to have an educated ministry, or should the free flow of the Spirit be accepted? Should the Christian message be presented as a "stone
fallen from heaven," or should concession be made to the
human situation and the message be told in a language understandable to the particular age even at the price of omitting
parts of that message? These questions, most of which are
familiar to all, cannot be answered to any degree here. It
is intended only that such questions be asked and an attempt
be made to answer them in the light of the rebellion motif.
Were some of these attitudes and actions rebellions, and if so,
which of them? And if any of them reveals itself as a rebellion, repentance should be made, responsibility accepted, and
a vow made that such a rebellion will never occur again.

If this is done, it will be seen that some of these attitudes
and actions were rebellions at a certain time and under certain circumstances, and others of them always were. Or, perhaps, in all of them always there was an element of rebellion.
Yet in no case should the final and most blessed message of
the motif, the unconditional grace of God, be forgotten. It
should never be forgotten that the history of God's people is
not simply a series of divine saving acts, but that these saving
acts were the results of continuous forgiveness, that the life
of God's people rests not merely on divine help, but on help
in spite of human rebellion. If this is accepted, with the admission that even in this acceptance there may be some bit
of rebellion—e.g., the lust for self-preservation—then the

church can never lose courage. For undoubtedly the Lord will do the same for the New Israel as he did for the Old:

> He remembered for their sake his covenant,
>> and relented according to the abundance of his steadfast love
>> (Ps. 106:45).

NOTES

1. INTRODUCTION

1. Friedrich Heiler, *Erscheinungsformen und Wesen der Religion* (Stuttgart, 1961), pp. 181, 482 ff.

2. These passages illustrate what might happen, according to the Old Testament, if the "power" is lost. The term used to denote the "power" in the Old Testament is "holiness." Cf. Lev. 2:3; 6:17 ff., 27. Of course, it denotes "material holiness."

3. Even the sin with Baal-Peor (Num. 25) is not ethical primarily. It is adultery, but it is either adultery committed with cult prostitutes or it is ritual promiscuity practiced by the Canaanites to achieve union with the goddess of fertility, represented by the female partner.

4. James B. Pritchard, ed., *Ancient Near Eastern Texts Relating to the Old Testament* (Princeton: Princeton University Press, 1950), p. 320.

5. E. A. Speiser, in Robert C. Dentan, ed., *The Idea of History in the Ancient Near East* (New Haven: Yale University Press, 1955), p. 56.

6. Gerhard von Rad, *Genesis: A Commentary* (The Old Testament Library; Philadelphia: The Westminster Press, 1961), pp. 13 ff.

7. von Rad, *Old Testament Theology* (New York: Harper & Brothers, 1962), Vol. I, pp. 115-121, 126-128.

8. *Ibid.*, p. 119.

9. G. Ernest Wright, *God Who Acts* (Chicago: Henry Regnery Company, 1952), p. 128.

10. Wright and R. H. Fuller, *The Book of the Acts of God* (Garden City, N.Y.: Doubleday & Company, 1957), pp. 20 ff., 28, 39.

11. von Rad, *Old Testament Theology*, Vol. I, pp. 56-68, 129-135.

12. Claus Westermann, *The Praise of God in the Psalms* (Richmond: John Knox Press, 1965), pp. 81-93.

13. von Rad, *Old Testament Theology*, Vol. I, p. 135.

14. The literary problems of the Pentateuch and of the Deuteronomic History are complicated; the scholarly disputes and the formulation of new theories will, probably, never come to an end. It is

impossible anymore to follow the development, the forward movement
of literary tradition, in detail; neither is the method of the compilers
fully understandable to the modern Western mind. Only the main out-
lines of the process seem to be certain. It is generally agreed that the
Pentateuch is a compilation of more sources, traditions, or documents.
Samuel Sandmel even holds that the "documents" are rather haggadic
expansions ("The Haggada Within Scripture," *Journal of Biblical
Literature* [hereafter abbreviated *JBL*], 1961, p. 105; more recently
in his book *The Hebrew Scriptures* [New York: Alfred A. Knopf,
1963]. For the sake of those who are less versed in Pentateuchal
literary analysis, let it be noted here that according to more or less
general scholarly agreement, first a document or tradition was created
called the *Yahwist* (scholarly symbol J), ca. 900-800 B.C. To this
from another source the *Elohist* material was added (symbol E, ca.
800-700), thus creating the *Yehovist* (JE). This work, in turn, was
combined with the *Deuteronomist* (D, ca. 650), the result of which
was JED. The last compilation was made by a priestly writer(s) who
added the *priestly material* (P, ca. 400). The end result was JEDP,
the Pentateuch, i.e., the Jewish Torah, the first five books of the Old
Testament. (For a modern version of the theory see Otto Eissfeldt,
The Old Testament: An Introduction [New York: Harper & Row,
1965], pp. 239-241.) The same principles are behind the theory about
the origins of the Deuteronomic History except that the assumed documents and sources are more numerous. The reasons that I speak about
the Tetrateuch (Gen., Exod., Lev., Num.) as a work which originally
had nothing to do with Deuteronomy are given, mainly in agreement
with Martin Noth (*Überlieferungsgeschichtliche Studien,* Berlin, 1938),
briefly in my article "The Book of the Conquest," *JBL,* 1965, p. 374.
With Eissfeldt's opinion that already in J's time there was a work
which told the story from creation to the age of the narrator, and
that the Pentateuch and those books which I—in agreement with
Noth—ascribe to the Deuteronomic History, constituted one great
work (Eissfeldt, *op. cit.,* pp. 241-248), I cannot agree. The present
text of Deuteronomy shows that it and the Tetrateuch were separate
works. Deut. 32:48-52 and the greater part of Deut. 34 are P material,
the former being a version of Num. 27:12-14, whereas no P material
is found in the Deuteronomic corpus itself (cf. von Rad, *Deuteronomy:
A Commentary,* The Old Testament Library, 1966). More important
is, however, that the view of history and the theology of the Tetrateuch
on the one hand, and of Deuteronomy, or rather of the Deuteronomic
History, on the other, are vastly different. I agree, however, fully
with Eissfeldt that any opinion concerning the literary history of the
Pentateuch will remain always a theory, and that not the theories are
important but that, according to the now unquestionable results of

Old Testament scholarship, the material in the Pentateuch is the result of more than one thousand years of literary activity.

15. Sandmel, *JBL,* 1961, p. 121.

16. Cf. Ezra 10:2-5; Neh. 9-10. Other passages where covenant repetitions are mentioned are: Deut. 29:1; Joshua 24; 2 Sam. 7; 2 Kings 11:17; 23:3; Jer. 31:31; Ezek. 16:60; 37:26 ff. These passages show that according to the Deuteronomic History whenever a complete breach of the fellowship between the Lord and the people (sometimes represented by the king) occurred, or whenever Israel faced a new situation, a covenant repetition was in place. It was the most effective means of restoring or strengthening that fellowship.

17. It is perhaps too early to draw conclusions, yet some observations in more recent literature may indicate that, in presenting a design for the restoration, the Tetrateuch had in mind also the remnants of the northern tribes, thus aiming to the full restoration of Israel. Moses Aberbach and Leivy Smolar (*JBL,* 1967, pp. 129 ff.) contend that the story of the golden calf, because it is an obvious reference to the "sin of Jeroboam the son of Nebat" (1 Kings 12:28 ff.), shows that the Aaronide priesthood was originally connected with the north and that the Zadokite priesthood of Jerusalem adopted Aaronide descent later (p. 138). In this story an attempt is made to soften the attack made upon Aaron by southern circles, inasmuch as he is represented as acting under popular pressure (Exod. 32:21 ff.). Moreover, Yohanan Aharoni, in his report on the Arad temple (*The Biblical Archaeologist,* 1968, p. 25), finds it probable that "not only the proportions but perhaps also the dimensions of the tabernacle were twenty by six cubits, exactly as the *hekal* at Arad." He also finds that the altar and the contents of the Arad temple "correspond to the biblical description of the tabernacle." In spite of one fundamental difference (the entrance of the tabernacle was on a shorter side, while the entrance of the Arad temple is on a longer side), he tentatively concludes: "it seems to me that the Arad temple was initially built in accordance with the plan of the tabernacle, and that this was the basic plan of all early Israelite temples."

If this tentative opinion of Aharoni proves true, then, taking into consideration the significance of archetypal patterns in the ancient world, it may lead us to the conclusion—to the embarrassment of many of us, I admit—that the Tetrateuch did not intend the rebuilding of the Jerusalem temple at all, but had in mind a portable sanctuary, the tabernacle. This would make the plan of the Tetrateuch, at least as far as the sanctuary was concerned, appear theoretical. But we must not forget that, as is generally admitted, the design of Ezekiel was also a theory which, when the restoration became a reality, was also totally disregarded. Apparently, before "Israel" could return, there were many dreams about the new life of the nation. Then, putting the two together—the opinion that the acceptance of Aaron was a concession to the north and the opinion of Aharoni—one might conclude that the Tetrateuch was the result of a compromise between the Jerusalem community, or of circles preceding it, and the remnants of the northern tribes, the precursors of the Samaritans.

Perhaps other considerations may also be mentioned here. The Tetrateuch does not refer expressly to either Jerusalem or the Davidic dynasty. Salem, where Melchizedek was priest and king may, of course, be a cover name for Jerusalem (Gen. 14:18). In the Jerusalem tradition the two cities were certainly identified, and the Davidic kings probably claimed the same type of kingship Melchizedek had (Ps. 110:4). Yet, strangely enough, in the text adopted by the Tetrateuch, Salem stands and not Jerusalem. Was the name changed in order to omit all reference to Jerusalem? Then the "place" Abraham saw in the land of Moriah (Gen. 22:4), which is identified by 2 Chron. 3:1 with the Jerusalem temple hill, does not necessarily refer to Jerusalem. As is known, the Samaritans claimed that Mount Moriah was identical with Gerizim. The Chronicler, whose work, it is generally accepted, was a polemic against the Samaritans, may have made the identification as a point against them. It is doubtful that the reference to the "star" from Jacob and the "scepter" from Israel (not from Judah! Num. 24:17) is to David. There could have been other kings, and they in the north, who could "crush the forehead of Moab." After all, this nation was under northern rule until the death of Ahab (2 Kings 3:5). Last but not least, it is certain that the Samaritans never would have accepted the Pentateuch as their Torah, as they did, had they known that its larger part, the Tetrateuch, was written only with the Jerusalem community in mind. Although I admit that further research is necessary at this point, it is difficult for me to deny that northern circles had a hand in the composition of the Tetrateuch.

18. Eissfeldt, *op. cit.*, pp. 210-212.
19. Sandmel, *op. cit.*, pp. 118 f.
20. The following classification of the material in the Tetrateuch according to these themes does not claim perfection. It is only for the purpose of illustration.
1. Gen. 1:1—12:3.
2. Gen. 12:4-9; 13; 15-18; 21:1-21; 22-24; 25:1-26; 26:1-5, 17-25; 28:10-17; 29:31-35; 30:1-24; 35:9-15; 36; Exod. 3:7-8; Num. 1:1—3:43; 26.
3. Gen. 12:10-20; 14; 19-20; 21:22-34; 25:27-34; 26:6-16; 27; 28:1—35:8, 16-29; 37-50; Exod. 13:17—14:9, 19-31; 15:1-21, 25-27; 16:13-36; 17:8-16; 23:23-33; 33:1—34:9; Num. 10:11-36; 20:14-21; 21:1-3, 10-35; 22-24; 27:12-23; 32:1—35:15.
4. Exod. 1-11; 12:29-42.

5. Exod. 19; 24; 34:10-35.
6. Gen. 32:32; 35:1-4; Exod. 18; 20:1—23:22; Lev. 11-15; 17-22; 24:10-23; 26-27; Num. 5-7; 20:22-29; 27:1-11; 30-31; 35:16-34; 36.
7. Gen. 22; 28:18-22; Exod. 12:1-28, 43-51; 13:1-16; 15:25b-26; 25-31; 35-40; Lev. 1-10; 16; 23:1—24:9; 25; Num. 3:44—4:49; 8:1—10:10; 15; 18-19; 20:22-29; 28:29.

21. Albrecht Alt, *Kleine Schriften zur Geschichte des Volkes Israel*, Vol. II (München, 1964), p. 328.

22. Neh. 4:1 ff., 7. *Ibid.*, p. 39.

23. Among many other authors, see Artur Weiser, *The Psalms: A Commentary* (The Old Testament Library; Philadelphia: The Westminster Press, 1962), pp. 36 ff.; J. Kraus, *Die Königsherrschaft Gottes* (Tübingen, 1951), pp. 30 ff.; Keith R. Crim, *The Royal Psalms* (Richmond: John Knox Press, 1962), *passim;* Sigmund Mowinckel, *The Psalms in Israel's Worship* (New York: Abingdon Press, 1962), Vol. I, pp. 106 ff.

24. von Rad, *Old Testament Theology*, Vol. I, p. 111.

25. Walther Eichrodt, *Theology of the Old Testament*, Vol. I (The Old Testament Library; Philadelphia: The Westminster Press, 1961), p. 512.

26. W. W. Jaeger, *The Theology of the Early Greek Philosophers* (Oxford: Clarendon Press, 1947), *passim.*

27. Paul M. van Buren, *The Secular Meaning of the Gospel* (New York: The Macmillan Company, 1963), pp. 131 ff.

2. The Motif of the Rebellions of Israel in the Tetrateuch

1. Pritchard, *op. cit.*, p. 119.

2. Martin Noth, *The History of Israel* (New York: Harper & Brothers, 1958), pp. 110 ff., esp. p. 36, n. 2; John Bright, *A History of Israel* (Philadelphia: The Westminster Press, 1959), pp. 114 ff., 124 ff.

3. Gerardus van der Leeuw, *Religion in Essence and Manifestation: A Study in Phenomenology* (London: Allen & Unwin, 1938), pp. 423 ff.

4. Was Moses' hesitancy to obey the Lord's commission to lead Israel out from Egypt a rebellion? To be sure, not in the strict sense of the word. I admit that in certain contexts in this book the term is too strong, yet for the sake of uniformity I denote as a rebellion every attitude of unwillingness to participate in the realization of the Lord's saving plan.

5. Sandmel calls the explanation of the name a "good-natured pun" (*JBL*, 1961, p. 113).

6. Was the story about Miriam's rebellion directed against Ezekiel? We have no positive evidence. Ezekiel—or whoever is responsible for chapers 40-48 in his book—presents the plans for the restoration of

the temple, the cult, the priesthood, and the division of the land as prophetic revelation. His ideas, however, do not agree with the Tetrateuch. He is also very strong in stressing that only the Zadokites among the Aaronides can be priests (40:46; 44:1 ff., 15 ff.), which is in sharp contrast to the Tetrateuch. As is known, Ezekiel's theory was never put into practice, and that was probably due to the resistance of the P circles or rather the circles in which the Tetrateuch originated. Was this rejection due to a compromise with the north, the Samaritans, where, possibly, the Aaronides held the priestly office? (Aberbach and Smolar, "Aaron, Jeroboam, and the Golden Calves," *JBL,* 1967, p. 129.) One is inclined to accept this opinion, considering the doubtless conciliatory attitude of the Tetrateuch, especially the fact that it does not mention either Jerusalem as the central sanctuary or the Davidic dynasty. At any rate, in the Miriam story the Tetrateuchal author lays down the principle: No law contradicting the "Mosaic," i.e., the Tetrateuchal, tradition is valid, even if it comes from the mouth of a prophet such as Ezekiel, who was, after all, of lower standing than the sister of Moses. From this it can be seen that there was no perfect agreement among those who prepared programs for the restoration.

3. The Emergence of the Rebellion Motif in History

1. S. J. De Vries derives the "murmuring tradition" (*JBL,* 1968, pp. 51 ff.), i.e., what I mean by the "rebellion motif," from "the theological reflex that faced the necessity of calibrating the southern conquest tradition with the already dominant tradition of the central ampictyony" (*ibid.,* p. 58). He is, of course, concerned only with the forward movement of tradition and makes no mention of the selective activity of the Tetrateuchal author. Apart from his unjustifiable exegesis (he forcibly misinterprets Num. 21:1-3, p. 57), it is to be questioned seriously whether the manifold and complicated motif of Israel's rebellions can be derived from such a "theological reflex."

2. For a rock actually yielding water in the desert, see G. Ernest Wright, *Biblical Archaeology* (Philadelphia: The Westminster Press, 1957), p. 65.

3. Frank E. Eakin, Jr., "Yahwism and Baalism Before the Exile," *JBL,* 1965, p. 407.

4. John Gray, *The Legacy of Canaan* (Leiden: E. J. Brill, 1965), pp. 163 ff.

5. Wright, *Biblical Archaeology,* p. 117.

6. The attack of G. Fohrer, and of other scholars, against the theory that there was a confederacy of the tribes before the monarchy (*Theologische Literaturzeitung,* 1966, col 801), must be considered as unsuccessful. If one takes the time and effort to set in two separate columns the pros and cons of the theory, the pros are overwhelming. Of course, from the present Old Testament one cannot expect an

elaborate description of this ancient organization. Both the Deuteronomic History and the Tetrateuch were written after the confederacy
ceased to exist, and with very little exception, even the earliest sources
of these two great works come from the time of the monarchy or
monarchies when the confederacy was in the process of dissolution.
But the traces can be found reliably in the present text. The pre-
cariousness of Fohrer's attack becomes clear if we consider that certain ideas outlived the confederacy. To mention only some, one idea
is the northern theory that each king must be called by the Lord as
all charismatic leaders; another is that Israel must have twelve tribes
and that there must be a central sanctuary. One wonders whether certain ideas of the Tetrateuch—in its present form a post-exilic work—
can be understood without assuming that its author reached back to
the traditions of the confederacy. It would be possible to mention more
than one idea, but one must suffice: As is well known, the Tetrateuch
never speaks about Jerusalem as the city of the central sanctuary.
The tradition which combines the land of Moriah with Mount Moriah
in Jerusalem (Gen. 22:2; 2 Chron. 3:1) is late, and the name in
Gen. 22 may be a scribal correction (H. Gunkel, *Genesis*). The
Tetrateuch never speaks of Jerusalem, and never refers to it even
cryptically. When it was compiled, this must have been known to all.
If its intention was to make the Jerusalem temple the central sanctuary,
and had that intention been known, the Samaritans would never have
accepted it as their sacred scripture. Late Samaritan tradition identified Moriah with Shechem with the same right as the Jews identified
it with the temple hill in Jerusalem. Scholarly opinion still holds that
the tabernacle is a movable copy of the temple of Jerusalem. As far
as its plan goes, this is certain, but the Tetrateuch never says that the
temple must be in Jerusalem. Unfortunately, it is impossible to reconstruct the theory of the Tetrateuch concerning the central sanctuary
for the time after the restoration. However, this much is clear: Its
author did not envisage the restoration of Judah alone but of all
twelve tribes. Did he also expect a movable central sanctuary? Perhaps he did. Of course, this again would be a contradiction of Ezekiel's
plan. But if such was the intention of the author, where did he find
this theory unless in the ancient tradition of the confederacy?

7. Gray, *op. cit.*, pp. 161, 198 ff., 212, 216, 242 ff. Arvid Kapelrud,
The Ras Shamra Discoveries and the Old Testament (Norman: University of Oklahoma Press, 1963), *passim*.

8. Albrecht Alt, "The Origins of Israelite Law," *Essays on Old
Testament History and Religion* (New York: Doubleday & Company,
1966), pp. 97-98.

9. M. Tsevat, *A Study of the Language of the Biblical Psalms*,
Monograph Series, *JBL*, 1955.

10. Pritchard, *op. cit.*, p. 279.

11. As, for example, Akhnaton, the "heretic" pharaoh, had changed his capital from Thebes to a site called today Tell-el-Amarna, indicating the introduction of the Aton worship.

12. Noth, *The History of Israel*, p. 240.

13. According to 2 Chron. 21:2 ff., Jehoram, the husband of Athaliah, also killed all his brothers.

14. Bright, *op. cit.*, p. 225.

15. Alt, "Das Gottesurteil auf dem Karmel," *Kleine Schriften*, Vol. II, pp. 141 ff.

16. Noth, *The History of Israel*, p. 192, tells us that this area was conquered only by David. The city of Jezreel was at the southeastern corner of the plain and had Israelite inhabitants (1 Kings 21:1).

17. Noth, *The History of Israel*, p. 266.

18. Isa. 2:6, 8, 18; Jer. 2:5 ff., 20 ff.; ch. 3; 4:1; 7:9; 10:1 ff.; 11:6 ff., 18; 18:14 ff.; 19:41 ff.; 44:15 ff.; Ezek. 23; Mic. 1:7; 5:10 ff.; Zeph. 1:4 ff.

4. THE MEANING OF THE REBELLION MOTIF

1. Mircea Eliade, *The Myth of the Eternal Return* (New York: Pantheon Books, 1954), *passim*, and *Patterns in Comparative Religion* (New York: Sheed & Ward, 1958), pp. 33, 395; K. Kerényi, *Umgang mit Göttlichem* (Göttingen, 1955), pp. 52 ff. Ulrich W. Mauser, in *Christ in the Wilderness* (London: SCM Press, 1963), thinks that Jesus' withdrawals to the wilderness meant new confrontations with the evil power and strengthening by God, that the wilderness motif in the New Testament is accompanied by the idea of final deliverance, and all this mirrors the sojourn of Israel in the wilderness. If this is true—and Mauser's line of argument is very attractive—we have an interesting belief that Jesus' and the church's life repeat the archetypal period of Israel. In other words, new sojourn in the wilderness means the beginning of a new, now final, archetypal age.

2. John A. MacCulloch, ed., *The Mythology of All Races*, vol. 8 (New York: Cooper Square Publishers, 1964), pp. 33 ff.; C. M. Schröder, ed., *Die Religionen der Menschheit* (RM) (Stuttgart), the following volumes: O. Zerris, *Die Religionen der Naturvölker Südamerikas und Westindiens*, vol. 7, 1959, pp. 283, 285; W. Krickeberg, *Die Religionen der Naturvölker Mesoamerikas*, vol. 7, pp. 100 ff.; I. Paulson, *Die Religionen der Nordasiatischen Völker*, vol. 3, p. 50; Åke Hultkrantz, *Die Religionen der Amerikanischen Arktis*, vol. 3, pp. 377 ff.; Ernst Dammann, *Die Religionen Afrikas*, vol. 6, 1963, p. 36.

3. van der Leeuw, *op. cit.*, pp. 414 ff.

4. A. M. Hocart, *The Life-Giving Myth* (New York: Humanities Press, 1952), pp. 12 ff.

5. S. Morenz, *Aegyptische Religion*, RM, 1960, p. 20.

6. Pritchard, *op. cit.*, pp. 60 ff.

7. Samuel H. Hooke, *Babylonian and Assyrian Religion* (Norman: University of Oklahoma Press, 1963), pp. 52 ff.; E. O. James, *Seasonal Feasts and Festivals* (New York: Barnes & Noble, 1961), pp. 80 ff.

8. Apparently, the archetype of covenant repetitions in Israel was the Sinai covenant. Cf. n. 16, ch. 1.

9. E.g., in the tracts *Yomah* and *Kodashim*.

10. S. Smith, "The Practice of Kingship in Early Semitic Kingdoms," in S. H. Hooke, *Myth, Ritual, and Kingship* (Oxford: Clarendon Press, 1958), p. 27.

11. Hooke, *Middle Eastern Mythology* (Baltimore: Penguin Books, 1963), p. 73.

12. In Exod. 24:6-8 we read about a covenant-making sacrifice offered by Moses. He threw half of the blood against the altar, the other half on the people. This is a communion-creating, a consecratory sacrifice in which the blood of the victim confers the holiness from the Lord upon the people the first time.

13. See n. 22, ch. 1.

14. In the Sermon of Benares the Buddha declares several times that the new knowledge he proclaims was not in tradition; it arose in him. This is the proclamation of a new revelation except that he does not, he cannot, name the god from whom it came, because for him the divine was impersonal or, at least, ineffable.

15. Eichrodt, *op. cit.*, pp. 45-56.

5. THE REBELLION MOTIF OUTSIDE THE TETRATEUCH

1. The reference to Moses' impatience in Deut. 32:51 is not part of the Book of the Conquest. It is P material, interpolated when Deuteronomy was made part of the Torah.

2. Eichrodt, *Der Prophet Hesekiel,* Das Alte Testament Deutsch (ATD), Vol. I (Göttingen, 1959).

3. *Ibid.*

4. It seems that in the Deuteronomic History the tradition of the *spotless generation* was in the offing but was never developed fully. This generation was the generation of the conquest which by Ezekiel is considered sinful. According to the Deuteronomic History, in this generation only two rebellions occurred but both were punished severely. One was the sin of Baal-Peor, the other the sin of Achan (Deut. 4:3 ff.; Joshua 7); otherwise they are praised several times or act faultlessly, as in Joshua 1:16; 22:16, 24 ff.; Judg. 2:10; cf. Jer. 2:2. According to this tradition, therefore, the generation of the conquest is a positive archetype. To Ezekiel the tradition is unknown.

5. In ancient times all names were *program names,* i.e., names which prefigured the future life and accomplishments of the bearer (e.g., Abraham's name means father of a multitude, Gen. 17:5). When he accomplished what his name suggested, the accomplishments were recited in a story, ballad, or praise, and that was the *story name.* Some praises and Psalms are the story names of the Lord (Exod. 15; Pss. 105; 136). Now, uttering the name, simple or story, over something meant that its owner took possession of the thing. (Cf. K. Galling, "Die Ausrufung des Namens als Rechtsakt in Israel," *Theol. Literaturzeitung,* 1956, col. 66). Thus the recitation of the Lord's story name meant that by it he came into the possession of the nations, or his hold on them was strengthened. On the other hand, if no accomplishment could be narrated or the person was unsuccessful, and that was known publicly, his name lost its power. The loss of fame, therefore, would have been a serious thing, because by that the Lord would have lost his hold over the nations.

6. Eichrodt thinks that it was a question whether they might initiate a sacrificial service in Babylonia (*Der Prophet Hesekiel,* ATD, Vol. II, 1966, p. 178).

7. Mowinckel, *op. cit.,* Vol. II, pp. 111 ff.

8. There is a reference to an obscure rebellion of the Ephraimites in Ps. 78:9, who "armed with the bow, turned back on the day of battle." Is this a Judean version of the story of the spies? There are indications that the author of the Psalm knew a tradition about the rebellions different from the Tetrateuch. This is shown by the question of the people in vs. 19, asked before the miracle of the quails and the manna, a question not known to the Tetrateuch.

9. van der Leeuw, *op. cit.,* p. 424.

10. Cf. n. 16, ch. 1.

11. In Ezra 10:3, which most probably speaks about the same occasion, the word *berith* is used.

12. The full form of the ancient Near Eastern treaties is discussed in G. Mendenhall, "Covenant Forms in Israelite Tradition," *Biblical Archaeologist,* 1954, No. 3. No covenant repetition in the Old Testament has the full form. They are *word covenants,* i.e., they have only three elements: the preamble (not always given), curse and oath, and the stipulations. The Moab covenant (Deut. 29:1) is a typical word covenant. It has the preamble (recitation of the saving acts of the Lord in the introductions to Deuteronomy), the famed curses in the epilogue, and the stipulations in the Deuteronomic laws. The different order of the elements from the Hittite treaties shows that Israel did not copy blindly the form of those treaties but drew on the same common tradition of ancient Near Eastern culture as the Hittites did. Another typical word covenant is described in the passage under discussion.

13. (1) Prohibition of Mixed Marriages, 10:30; (2) The Sabbath, vs. 31a; (3) The Sabbatical Year, vs. 31b; (4) The Temple Tax, vss. 32 f.; (5) Wood for Sacrifices, vs. 34; (6) First Fruits, vss. 35-37a; (7) The Tithe, vss. 37b-39.

14. A tradition unknown to the Tetrateuch. Does this verse refer to the story of the spies? The Tetrateuch knows only of the intention to appoint a leader (Num. 14:4). If the verse speaks about the spies, the order of the events is not the same as in the Tetrateuch.

15. References in the text to *Gaster* are made to Theodor H. Gaster, tr., *The Dead Sea Scriptures* (Garden City, N.Y.: Doubleday Anchor Books, 1964). I have used this text because it is easily available.

6. THE SIGNIFICANCE OF THE REBELLION MOTIF FOR THE NEW ISRAEL

1. This was the reaction of a member of the audience when I read the paper from which the present book grew.

2. Calvin, *Institutes*, II.I.6.

3. Rudolf Otto, *The Idea of the Holy, passim.*

4. John Oman, *The Natural and the Supernatural* (New York: The Macmillan Company, 1931), p. 366.

5. Augustine, *City of God*, XIX.13.

6. Such acceptable philosophizing is Willem F. Zuurdeeg's *An Analytical Philosophy of Religion* (New York: Abingdon Press, 1958), or Paul M. van Buren's book *The Secular Meaning of the Gospel*, or the article of H. Gollwitzer, "Das Wort 'Gott' in Christlicher Theologie," *Theol. Lit. Zeitung*, 1967, col. 161. Such pursuits, besides giving great delight, serve the important purpose of conveying, without adulteration, the meaning of the Christian truth to those who otherwise would have no ear for it.

7. *Confessions*, IV.12.19; *Ev. Joh. Tract*, XXVI.4.

8. David Hume, *An Enquiry Concerning Human Understanding*, Sec. X, Part II; *A Treatise of Human Nature*, I.1.6. George F. Thomas, *Religious Philosophies of the West* (New York: Charles Scribner's Sons, 1965), in his chapter on Hume and especially pp. 219 ff., misses Hume's point and does not see his true and very important contribution to Christian theology. Hume was a skeptic only toward metaphysics and philosophical theology; he was a Christian believer.

9. Kant, *Prolegomena to Any Future Metaphysic*, Third Part. III. §55; *Critique of Pure Reason*, §§249, 253.

10. Oman was professor and principal of Westminster College, Cambridge, England. The reason he is not generally known (however, see John Hick, *Faith and Knowledge* [Ithaca: Cornell University Press, 1957], p. xix) is, probably, the difficult style of his *magnum opus, The Natural and the Supernatural*. How hard it was to understand him is shown by the following true anecdote. He was a Scotchman with an

accent difficult to understand. As a visiting student with pitifully little
knowledge of the King's English and a little more than pitiful training
in philosophy, I tried to apprehend his deep lectures. After two weeks,
however, I gave up and complained to my English-born fellow students: "I just can't understand him." The answer was: "Never mind,
we don't either." As I believe now, the reason they could not understand him either was not so much the Scottish dialect but rather the
complicated structure of his sentences. Anyone who does not believe
this should read his book.

11. Carl G. Jung, *Collected Works,* vol. 11, *Psychology and Religion: West and East* (Princeton: Princeton University Press, 1958),
p. 551.

12. Both Tillich and Thomas J. J. Altizer (*The Gospel of Christian
Atheism* [Philadelphia: The Westminster Press, 1966]) are representatives of philosophical theology. As Oman also, they have at the basis
of their systems an overwhelming religious experience which they de-
scribe in philosophical terms. I have selected Oman because his system,
even though he, apparently, did not know anything about Martin
Buber, shows a remarkable similarity with Buber's thought. Compare
the initial sentence in *I and Thou* (2nd ed.)—"To man the world is
twofold, in accordance with his twofold attitude"—with Oman's sentence: "The two [the Natural and the Supernatural] are not in opposition, but are so constantly interwoven that nothing may be wholly
natural or wholly supernatural" (p. 72). Indeed, if one would substitute the *Thou* of Buber with the *Supernatural* of Oman, and the *It* of
the former with the *Natural* of the latter, one would discover the same
type of religious experience and a similar philosophical situation.

13. Edward John Carnell, *The Case for Orthodox Theology* (Philadelphia: The Westminster Press, 1959).

14. Daniel B. Stevick, *Beyond Fundamentalism* (Richmond: John
Knox Press, 1964), pp. 17 ff.

15. For brevity's sake I deal here only with the case of the New
Testament authors, but with a little change the same could be said
also about the authors of the Old Testament.

16. ". . . the written Word does not commend itself unless the
heart is confronted by the living Word" (Carnell, *op. cit.,* p. 33).

17. By "cultic" he probably means sectarian.